His Warrior Princess

A Girlfriend's Guide to Being Lit from Within

By Cheryl Wright

His Warrior Princess: A Girlfriend's Guide to Being Lit From Within
By Cheryl Wright
Copyright © 2020

ISBN: 978-1-7352648-0-6
E-book ISBN: 978-1-7352648-1-3

Cover Design by Olivia Wheelock – kilnliterary.com
Editor and Interior Design by Sarah Miles – kilnliterary.com

Cover Photo taken by Magen Marr

Dedication

To all the Warrior Princesses I have had the honor of knowing,
including my own daughter, mother, sister, sister-in-loves, faithful
friends, and those I have admired from afar—this study is dedicated
to you. May you continue to radiate His Glory.

*Living within you is the Christ who floods you with the expectation
of glory! This mystery of Christ, embedded within us, becomes a
Heavenly treasure chest of hope filled with the riches of glory for
His people, and God wants everyone to know it!*

– Colossians 1:27 (TPT)

Contents

Foreword 7

What's Your Story? 9

Girls with Gumption: Joan of Arc 19

Falling in Love with Jesus 21

Girls with Gumption: Corrie Ten Boom 35

How to Catch An Arrow 37

Girls with Gumption: Kathryn Kuhlman 53

What Am I Listening To? 55

Girls with Gumption: Aimee Semple McPherson 67

The Frequency, Sound, and Power of Our Words 69

Girls With Gumption: Evangeline Booth 81

Taking Every Thought Captive 83

Girls with Gumption: Jeanne Guyon 95

What are You Packing? 97

Girls with Gumption: Harriet Tubman 111

Book of Destiny 113

Girls with Gumption: Heidi Baker 125

What Is Our Identity? 127

Afterword: Dear Daughter 137

Endnotes 143

Foreword

A while ago, I attended my high school reunion; I'll refrain from stating which decade. In preparation for the reunion, I looked back through old yearbooks. I was especially drawn to the section which listed the seniors and what they were destined to become. "Destined to become president, destined to make a million dollars before they're 25, destined to find new uses for paper clips," and the surmising goes on. My yearbook stated I was destined to wear pink for the rest of my life. That's not too ambitious. I was destined for a lot more than that, however.

This book that you hold in your hands is a feeble attempt to peek into a destiny so beautiful and wondrous that it can scarcely be put into mere words. We are destined to unwrap our identity as a Warrior Princess who radiates the glory of God. You are indeed lit from within!

This book can be used a few ways. It can be a study read individually, allowing time to dialogue with God and journal the questions at the end of each chapter. It could also be read in a group and the huddle questions and activations done together. Finally, my daughter and I have done this study with a group as a mother-daughter collaboration. The girls and I (as the leader) would do a few chapters together over the course of a few weeks, then we would invite the mothers to join us and the girls would teach the mothers what they had learned from the previous chapters. We would usually share a meal together and the girls would take turns summarizing what they got out of each chapter. It was a powerful time of sharing what the Lord was speaking to us and allowed the mothers to interact with their daughters in ways they might not have before.

Are you ready to have some paradigms shifted? Are you ready to explore some potentially new territory? Our relationship with the Lord is a big adventure. Although He is the ultimate destination, one can never swish their hand across their forehead and declare they have arrived. That is the beauty of our pursuit of Him. Our relationship with Him is a journey we accept not knowing exactly where we are going, but it is a thrilling ride!

All that I know is that I have glimpsed a sliver of His glory and it propels me towards Him. I must know Him more. I have packed my bags and am on a journey deeper into His heart. Would you like to come? Let's begin.

1

What's Your Story?

"I am not afraid; I was born to do this."

– Joan of Arc

I've always loved a good story. My Grandfather used to tell the most fantastical stories that had my siblings, cousins, and me riveted on his every word. There was a dragon? Will it spew out fire over the fair maiden and her farmer? We would hold our breath as my Grandfather would envelope us in worlds of knights, castles, beanstalks, and the occasional princess or two. I remember driving for days to get to my Grandma and Grandpa's white house close to the Red River in Winnipeg, Manitoba. Flinging open the station wagon door, we'd run to the back of the house where his garden stood. He'd gently coax unbelievably large carrots out of the dark earth, wash them off with the hose, and we would crunch on them as he would start with, "Once upon a time . . ."

Stories have such power. They draw us in, coax out emotions, bond us together. Since the beginning of time they have been both a pastime and a place of community. Sharing stories inspires and encourages us. It makes us see others in a new light, and allows us to learn more about ourselves in the process. Why are stories so powerful? Well, because stories are a tool of God's revelation in this world. He Himself is a storyteller. In fact, God is the Teller of the grandest story—one of His relentless love for His people, you and me.

Everyone has a story. It can be the boring facts of where you grew up, what school you attend; or, it can be more complex, like what you like to do, or what you dream of for the future. Your story reveals a deeper peek into who you are, including your heart aches, struggles, and fears. All of our experiences, encounters, and hopes for the future are woven into the sometimes beautiful and sometimes heartbreaking story we are currently writing.

This study is called "His Warrior Princess" and my hope is that you will come with me on a journey of discovery into your identity as a princess who is deeply loved and passionately sought after by a God Who lovingly and uniquely created you. You are a warrior who is equipped and anointed to fight every battle which you encounter in life. Chances are, you may feel you have no idea who you are, who God is and how you are supposed to live life activated by His Joy and Presence every moment of the day. The journey of this book is meant to take you there, starting with understanding your own storyline. God has great and wonderful things for you ahead.

Warrior Princess, let me ask you—Do you know who you really are? Let me tell you—

You are in a battle for good and evil. In your story there is you—the hero princess—and there is an enemy who does not want you to discover your true identity. He wants to keep you locked in comparison: to others, to perfectionism in yourself, and to the unrealistic and false lives others create on social media. Your life is a battle. You battle your friends, your family, and yourself in an attempt to calm the anxiety and chaos that is your life. You battle your thought life, trying to quiet the lies that scream you are not enough, you will never measure up, and that you just better give up.

However, there is another character in your storyline, and He is your Rescuer Redeemer. His name is Jesus. The movie *Lord of the Rings: The Fellowship of the Ring*, based on J.R.R. Tolkien's book, was advertised with a phrase which said, "Fate Has Chosen Him. A Fellowship Will Protect Him. Evil Will Hunt Them." It succinctly paints a grand picture of destiny, struggle, and hope. You have that same destiny, but I'd like to amend it a bit: "God has chosen you.

Evil will hunt you; the Lord will protect you, and a fellowship or sisterhood will gather around you and cheer you on."

Why does every story have to have a villain; some type of adversity we come up against and must fight through? Even the best of fairy tales have villains: Maleficent, Cruella de Vil, White Witch of Narnia, Ursula, just to name a few. Your story has a villain, one who likes to remind you of everything you are not. He likes to steal, kill, and destroy everything in your life which is good, has meaning, or gives purpose. The enemy in our life is satan. He seeks to continuously antagonize and torment us in every area of your life where we give him access. 1 Peter 5:8 (TPT) tells us to "be well balanced and always alert, because [your] enemy, the devil, roams around incessantly, like a roaring lion looking for its prey to devour." Take a decisive stand against him and resist his every attack with strong, vigorous faith. That certainly sounds like something a heroic Warrior Princess would do! But more on the protagonist later (Hint: that's YOU!).

Every great story also has a rescue. It is the place in the story where the heroine has gotten into a pickle and needs some assistance before the villain hurts or destroys her. Sometimes the heroine becomes empowered by realizing who her rescuer really is, and who she really is. All she needs is a sword, gumption, and Someone to back her up. Who is the Rescuer in our story? He is the Author of Creation and the Designer of Our Story. He stepped out of eternity and into reality to become our Hero, our Knight in Shining Armor. He goes by many names, depending on the circumstance we're in. He could be Jehovah Jireh, my Provider when we don't know what to do. He is Emmanuel—God with us when we feel all alone; my Savior when we just don't know how to rise above our circumstances; King of Kings when we need to be reminded of His power and sovereignty over things that we can't fix. We need to understand that this Rescuer is Someone in love, and He came to rescue you.

Our hearts were made for "happily ever after," yet so many times there is not a happy-ever-after in the story of our lives. We find ourselves like a lost little girl, not knowing which way to turn or how our story is supposed to end. We fumble along our way, with eyes half-shut, trying to discern in which direction our happy ending is. I have good news! There is Someone Who is here to help.

In our story that Someone is Jesus. Jesus is our Protector, Burden-Bearer, Comforter, Confidence, Counselor, Deliverer, Ever-

Present Helper, Friend, Good Shepherd, Healer, Emmanuel, Joy, Overcomer, Prince of Peace, Quieter of the Storm, Refuge, Shield, Trustworthy, Unchanging, Understanding, Vindicator, and Wall of Fire. Those are just a few of the names He goes by! With each adventure or hardship we go through, we come to know Him by a new name. In the story of your life, He is your Rescuer Redeemer.

If that is who Jesus is in your story, then what does that make you?

Psalm 139:13-14 (TPT) says, "You formed my innermost being, shaping my delicate inside and my intricate outside, and wove them all together in my mother's womb. I thank you, God, for making me so mysteriously complex! Everything you do is marvelously breathtaking. It simply amazes me to think about it! How thoroughly you know me, Lord!"

"It takes courage to grow up and become who you really are."
– e e cummings

Do you know that you are "his poetry, a re-created people that will fulfill the destiny He has given each of us, for we are joined to Jesus, the Anointed One. Even before [you] were born, God planned in advance [your] destiny and the good works [you] would do to fulfill it!" (Ephesians 2:10 TPT).

Our identity is in Him. We are not the sum of what everyone else has said about us; we are not the sum of all the lies we think about ourselves; we are, at the end of the day, a daughter of God— chosen, accepted, and loved by Him. We need not seek the approval of others, for we are who He says we are. No one can take this away from us. Others may have rejected us, but He stands in front of you now, spreads His arms wide open, and says, "You are mine."

We may feel that we are not worthy of this type of love and recognition. God does not compare us to others and so we should not compare ourselves. He is not concerned with what the world thinks about us. We do not need to conform to a particular image the world has formed—the curated, photo shopped, snapchatted, filtered life which we put on Instagram. That is not reality; it is only what we choose for others to see.

He says in 1Samuel 16:7 (NASB), "God sees not as man sees, for man looks at the outward appearance, but the Lord looks at the heart." When He looks at us, He sees His wanted, chosen, precious treasure. We are not rejected and worthless as the villain in our story would have us believe, but rather our Rescuer tells us we are wanted, chosen, and accepted.

Why do we want others to notice us, to admire us, and to want to spend time with us? There is an inherent desire in us all to be loved—just loved. I want to be loved. You may have looked for love in all the wrong places to fulfill that longing to be accepted and cherished. Like Bridget Jones, we may want someone to love us "just as we are." Isn't it our heart's cry?

There is a Spanish story of a father and son who became estranged.[1] The son ran away and the father was frantic to find him. After much searching, he put an ad in the Madrid newspaper hoping his son would see it. It read "Dear Paco, meet me in front of the newspaper office at noon on Saturday. All is forgiven. I love you. Your Father." On Saturday, 800 Pacos showed up outside the newspaper office, searching for forgiveness and love from their fathers. No matter what we do to cover up the hurt, there is only one solution for the emptiness inside, and that is a revelation of—and emotional connection with—the heart of our Rescuer, Jesus. Exactly how much does the Creator of our story love us? Let's look at some facts about His love.

Fact 1: The Author of our story loves us unconditionally—He knows everything about us!

I always knew my own earthly father loved me when he would tell people the story of the day I was born. He absolutely loved to tell this story. I was his first child, and at the time I was born, the father wasn't allowed in the delivery room with the mother and the baby. But, he was so excited once he did get to see me and hold me, that he left the car at the hospital that day. He and mom took a cab back to the house so he could hold me all the way home. I felt so loved, and I loved hearing that story over and over again.

God loves us like that, but even more! God numbers even the hairs on our head, according to Matthew 10:30 (NASB). In Jeremiah 31:3 (NASB) he assures us "I have loved you with an everlasting love; therefore I have drawn you with lovingkindness." In Ephesians 3:18-19 (TPT), Paul talks of the breadth and length and height and depth of God's love. Not only is His love great for us, but He chose you to be the recipient of that love!

In Malachi 1:2 (NLT), our Rescuer says to us: "I have always loved you." That word love in Hebrew translates to mean "the unspeakable love and tender mercies of God in the covenant relationship with His people."[2] Numbers 14:19 (NASB) talks of His magnificent, unfailing love for us. You are loved. Ephesians 1:11-12 (TPT) says that He chose you when He planned creation. His love for us translates even into comfort—to be embraced in the Father's arms. Feeling like your life is in too much of a mess for the Lord to understand what you are going through? Psalm 34:18 (NASB) says "The Lord is near to the brokenhearted, and saves those who are crushed in spirit." Just so you are further reassured, Psalm 147:3 (NASB) says, "He heals the brokenhearted and binds up their wounds." How awesome to have our Daddy swoop us up in His arms and hold us when we hurt. He can only do this if we allow Him to. Open yourself up to His embrace; allow the Holy Spirit to reveal the Lord's heart to you.

Fact 2: Once we receive God's love, nothing can separate us from it.

Romans 8:38-39 (NLT) says, "Nothing can ever separate us from God's love." What?! Who is this God that says He loves us in the midst of our chaos, our mess ups, and our insecurities? Romans 8:35 (KJV) says, "Who shall separate us from the love of Christ? Shall tribulation, or distress, or persecution, or famine, or nakedness, or peril or sword?" In verses 38 and 39 (NASB), Paul goes on to say, "For I am convinced that neither death, nor life, nor angels, nor principalities, nor things present, nor things to come, nor powers, nor height, nor depth, nor any other created thing shall be able to separate us from the love of God which is in Christ Jesus our Lord."

The villain in our story has been lying to us. Have you ever felt that you are so unworthy of God's love that you can't believe He would love you this intensely? God isn't mad at us; He isn't sitting in Heaven waiting for us to mess up and hit us over the head when we do. He is in love with us and His love for us does not change. He sees our story unfolding and He is there on every page, watching us, waiting for us to invite Him into the storyline. We cannot believe and agree with the lies of the villain; we must cut ourselves free from those lies that bind us up and tie us down so that we can actively participate in the incredible dramatic story the Lord has for our lives.

> *"For he has rescued us from the dominion of darkness and brought us into the kingdom of the Son he loves, in whom we have redemption, the forgiveness of sins."*
> *(Colossians 1:13 NIV)*

Our story has us playing the part of the heroine, God as our Rescuer/Redeemer, and a villain whose sole intent is to destroy our happily ever after. Our hero, Jesus, is in need of Warrior Princesses who know who they are, know the authority they have, know the beauty they possess, and know the damage to the enemy's kingdom they can inflict. He needs His heroines free from the shackles of the lies of the villain. He wants us to take up our swords and plunge His truth into every lie that has held us back. He whispers to you "Your glory is needed, what say you?"

So, who is this Warrior Princess?

Is she some type of super hero, girl power, cape-and-tiara-wearing, fierce beauty? Is she someone who understands exactly who she is and is comfortable in her identity as a Daughter of the Most High God? Is she a scared girl who is learning how to be a brave follower of Jesus? Well, I think she is all of the above. A Warrior Princess is an equipped, anointed friend of God who desires to fulfill the destiny she was created for. She is not perfect or fearless; but, she is on a journey with her hand held by the One who flung the stars in space. He never leaves her and His goodness never fails her.

That is you, whether you feel like it or feel like that could never be what anyone calls you. Let me tell you who this girl is: She is who you were created to be! You are a fierce, weapon-wielding, demon-slaying, river-of-life-riding, sword-toting, blood-bought, God-fragranced, stunningly beautiful daughter of the Most High God. That my friend is who you really are! Still don't believe it? That's ok. That is why we are on this journey together.

You were born for such time as this, and you are equipped and anointed. You can learn to hear His voice, develop a relationship with Him, know the friendship of Holy Spirit—in essence, you've got this! You can do it! You are the Warrior Princess in the story of your life. You are wanted, chosen, equipped, and desired in the grand story that is your life. Let's get ready! No, wait a minute, you were born ready!

Prayer:

Lord, I may have done things that I feel disqualify me from Your love. I ask forgiveness right now for those sins. You took the punishment for those sins on the Cross and I receive Your forgiveness now. Open my eyes so I can see myself as You see me. Open my ears to hear Your Voice which tells me who I really am. Illuminate Your Word to me so I can understand Who You are. I want to know You more deeply. Teach me, Holy Spirit, and bring me to a place of deep understanding of my worth, my identity, and my authority in You. I am ready! In Jesus' name, Amen.

Activation:

Daughter, you were born for such a time as this to impact the world, leave a legacy, and shape history with your courage. You may not exactly understand who you are or know the Lord very deeply, but you are on a journey to find out more. Take a deep breath and believe the truth that the God of the Universe wants you to know Him, and He really, really loves you. You are seen, you are valued, your strength is needed. Relax, He's got this. More importantly, He's got you!

Huddle Questions:

1. What do you want to get out of this study?

2. What is your favorite fairy tale story or Disney princess movie? What about it makes it your favorite?

3. If you were to write a senior yearbook description of a Warrior Princess, what would you write?

4. Do you see Jesus as your Rescuer and Redeemer? Why or why not?

Girls with Gumption: Joan of Arc

Joan of Arc was born around 1412 during a very dark time in France's history. Poverty and famine were rampant, and it was said that wolves would come into Paris at night to feed on bodies which were left unburied in the streets. From an early age Joan displayed an incredible love for the Lord. Joan would go to mass and God would meet her there. When she was 13, she had her first Heavenly encounter with the Lord, and the Lord began to give her dreams and visions of her leading an army. In the 1400s, women were not given leadership positions, so it was crazy to think this teenage girl would ever be put in charge of an army. But God had given Joan a vision that she was a Warrior Princess and Joan trusted God with that vision. Joan presented herself to the commander of armies who was in a neighboring town and told him she was reporting for duty. He laughed at her and sent her home. She was persistent and returned until they took a look at her incredible sword skills. She was granted an audience before future King Charles VII and he agreed that she could fight. Joan carried the presence of God and it drew people to her. Joan said "I have a vision from God. He has called me to raise an army for our nation and for Him."

As Joan became well known, soldiers wanted to fight by her side. To the rough and vulgar troops, she held up a standard and example of righteousness, purity, and devotion to God. They rallied around this curious girl with big dreams and conviction. She told the soldiers if they wanted to fight in her "army of the Lord," they had to get rid of the camp prostitutes, attend church every day, and stop swearing. Incredibly, the soldiers embraced these standards. Before they would go into battle, Joan would have everyone take communion. Joan had no military or strategy training, but God gave her battle plans on the field. April 30, 1429, 17-year-old Joan and her army entered the city of Orleans, and within a week had captured all the English forts around the city. Even though Joan was wounded by an arrow, she pressed on and captured the city of Troyes which led to victory. When Charles was crowned king, Joan stood by him as a witness.

Sadly, Joan was executed by the English for war crimes when she was 19. Twenty-five years later, she was declared innocent of all the crimes for which she was executed. Joan had a sword in her hand, heard God's voice, and knew the authority God gave her. She was His Warrior Princess.

2

Falling in Love with Jesus

"With the same intensity that the Father loves Jesus, He loves you."

– Mike Bickle, International House of Prayer Founder

What is one word people would say best describes you? Maybe you are quirky, caring, friendly, creative, kind, or perceptive. Think about a quality in a friend you are most drawn to. For some people, loyalty may be something that they value, for others it could be kindness. If you have a good friend you have known for a long time, you probably have a great word to describe them, along with a history of shared memories, funny circumstances and common experiences.

Recently my daughter and her friend created an Instagram account together that documented their friendship. A quick scroll through reveals tales of drive-through coffee runs, crazy selfies, and car karaoke videos. During their senior year of high school, what a sweet way to remember all the fun and sometimes challenging times friendship evokes. Both of their personalities come out in the pictures and captions, as they have allowed others a glimpse into their treasured times together. Their descriptions of each other are spot-on. I'm sure they would nail describing each other in one word! They know one another well because they have spent a lot of time together.

What word would the Lord use to describe you? Would it be the same one your friends use? We may have never thought it possible to have that type of deep relationship with the Lord. That is my desire. I want to have to have a close intimate relationship with the Lord. I want a history with Him. And I want that for you, too, my Warrior Princess!

> *"Move your heart closer and closer to God*
> *and He will come even closer to you."*
> *(James 4:8 TPT)*

Our desire to have a deep relationship with the Lord can be cultivated by spending time in His presence, knowing His personality, seeking His ways, and understanding what He loves about us. The more time we spend with Him, the better we come to know Him, to hear His voice, and to understand His mysteries. Ephesians 3:17-19 (AMP) says, "And may you, having been rooted and grounded in love, be fully capable of comprehending with all the saints the width and length and height and depth of His love; and may you come to know the love of Christ which far surpasses knowledge, that you may be filled up to all the fullness of God, completely filled and flooded with God Himself." Do we really comprehend the width, length, height, and depth of His love for us? That notion can make some feel uncomfortable—that this God of the Universe is madly in love with us. We may ask ourselves if we can even allow Him to love us in that depth, if we feel uncomfortable allowing others to even come close.

Sometimes during times of difficulty, we may find ourselves leaning in to the Lord, but other times, we keep Him firmly at arm's length. There are many reasons for this. Maybe we have felt He let us down, or did not answer a prayer the way we thought He would (or should!). We may even be annoyed with Him because of it. How do we move from viewing Him skeptically or warily to embracing Him as Someone we could potentially fall in love with? Sometimes we may hold friends at arm's length, leery of letting them come into the inner sanctum of our hearts for fear that they may take from us, reject us, or hurt us if they know too much about the real us. However, if we treat God that way, we will have a God-shaped hole in ourselves, as Pascal says. We were created for companionship with Him; we were created for intimacy.

What does intimacy with Jesus really mean?

I have a strange image for you to help explain what I mean by this kind of intimacy. Just . . . hang with me. I love fajitas, but rarely order them at a restaurant because I seem to have the most porous hair ever. As soon as a waiter walks by me with a sizzling plate of fajitas, the smell seems to be sucked up onto my hair and I can enjoy the smell of fajitas every time I swing my hair, until I wash the smell out. This interesting phenomenon works with campfire smoke as well. People can smell where I have been! I was thinking about that the other day and thought: Could that I absorb His beautiful fragrance when I spend time with Him? I would like to think that when I've spent time with Jesus, saturating and marinating in His presence, people can smell the fragrance of God on me. His fragrance doesn't necessarily take on a physical odor that you smell with your nose (like the plate of fajitas), but others can tell Who you've been spending time with. That time with Him reflects not only in our countenance, but in our words, actions, and thoughts. 2 Corinthians 2:15 (AMP) says, "For we are the sweet fragrance of Christ to God, among those who are being saved and among those who are perishing."

This fragrant intimacy with Jesus is the close relationship that is cultivated by spending time in His presence, and knowing His personality, His ways, His character. Just like our close friends, the more time we spend with Him, the better we come to know Him, to hear His voice, and to understand His mysteries. You may be wondering why we need this type of intimate relationship with Jesus. Well, the Creator wants to spend time with His creation. We, in turn, need to spend time with our Creator so that we can bloom into the person He dreamed we would be as He knit us in our mother's womb, fashioning us cell by cell. Our time spent in His Presence causes us to become more like Him.

Wanting a deep relationship with God was His true plan and hope for us all along. God created the world with the desire for a family that would voluntarily love Him and want to spent time with Him. The tragedy of the fall was that mankind sinned and gave his authority and rights away to the enemy; but even more heart wrenching was the absence of God's presence in the Garden. Before that, Adam and Eve enjoyed constant communication with the Lord. I wonder what would it have been like to commune with the Lord, Spirit to Spirit, to have no barriers, no difficulty hearing, and no miscommunication. What a loss of intimacy, indeed! But hope is not lost. God still wants intimacy with us, here and now in our own stories. He loves you—beyond measure—and wants you to fall in love with Him, too.

I remember an awkward time in my fourth-grade gym class when two team captains were chosen for a baseball game and the excruciating team-picking process began. Waiting to be picked was unbearable—thoughts like, *"Will I be picked next?"* and, *"Does anyone want me?"* swam in my anxious mind. It was uncomfortable as name after name was called and the students triumphantly joined the other chosen ones behind their team captain. It came down to three of us left waiting on the other side of the gym, staring into the faces of our classmates; some wore sneering faces, while a few faces had large eyes of sadness secretly supporting me in their countenance and hoping mine would be the next name called. Alas, I was not the third-to-last teammate. It came down to another student and I, and yet I was still not the next name called. I was the very last person picked. I remember that feeling of not being chosen, not being called, not being wanted. That sounds very dramatic, but I remember my fourth-grade heart hurt at the time. I am sure most of you can relate to that feeling, whether you were also picked last, or the star athlete of your class. The feeling of rejection and not being wanted is crushing.

But in Isaiah 41:9 (NASB), God tells us, "You whom I have taken from the ends of the earth, and called from its remotest parts and said to you, 'You are My servant, I have chosen you and not rejected you.'" Wow, He has chosen me. He has chosen you! Give that a minute to let it sink in. God not only wants you, he chose you specifically! He further hits this concept home by saying in John 15:16 (AMP), "You have not chosen Me, but I have chosen you and I have appointed and placed and purposefully planted you . . ." He wants you. He has chosen you. You have a seat at the table, an invite to the party. So how do we get to know Him better? How do we fall in love with the One who is so obviously in love with us?

> *He has chosen us as His creation to have a close relationship with Him. He wants you to want Him. He desires a Bride that will voluntarily love Him. He gave us free will and He wants us to choose Him in the same way we hope to be chosen.*

What does falling in love with God look like?

I love choosing just the right present for a dear friend; it is an act of love carefully pondering what they like or said they might need, and then putting the time in to select just the right gift that you know will bring them joy and pleasure. The deeper my understanding of that person, the more carefully I can select a gift that suits them.

We can choose the perfect gift because we really know our friend. However, we can say we "know" someone, but have no idea what gift to choose. That could be because we may know about them from afar but do not have a close, personal relationship with them. For example, I know the President—I know the position, some of its history, and about the person currently in office. But, if I were to go to the White House and we ran into each other, we would not truly know each other at all. Knowing about someone does not mean we know them. In the same way, knowing about God does not mean we have a deep, intimate relationship with Him.

While my husband was in university, he encountered a student from India who was about to enter an arranged marriage. My husband questioned how this man felt about having his family choose a wife for him. The man replied he was at peace and this was how things were done in his family for generations. But when it comes to Jesus, I don't want to get to Heaven and have to ask someone to point out Jesus to me. I want to be acquainted with Him, here and now, to the point that I can know Him and love Him. I want to know all about Him, to know His moods, His personality, His characteristics. I want to be on a face to face basis with Him.

But just how do we love God? Matthew 22:37 (NLT) says to "love the Lord your God with all your heart, all your soul, and all your mind." It is difficult to figure out how to love Him with our heart, soul, and mind. Sometimes we may wrestle with the question of whether we actually have the courage to love God like that, with our whole heart, soul, and mind. Do we try to give Him just a bit of ourselves, and keep the rest that needs to be cleaned up separated from God? We may reason we will keep a part of ourselves where we can do what we want and not have God mess with that part of our lives. This is not love as God wishes and designed for us. You fall deeply in love with someone when you have an understanding of who they are. Falling in love with God is the same thing. We need to know Him as He knows us.

We may not exactly know what God looks like, although there are plenty of "God sightings," called Theophanies, in the Word. However, we know how He interacts with us and others, His ways, His character, His emotions. Psalm 139:17-18 (NIV) shows us the joy of intimately knowing God: "How precious to me are your thoughts God! How vast is the sum of them? Were I to count them, they would outnumber the grains of sand—when I awake, I am still with you." If you have not been ignited with desire to know Him, maybe it is because you do not really have an understanding of Who He really is. This is why knowing is so important. I do not want to be only an acquaintance when it comes to Jesus. I want to know His smile, experience His nearness, and understand His personality. Knowing and loving go hand-in-hand. As you spend more time with God you will know Him and love Him more and more.

Falling in love: Say yes to more of Him.

We may have friends that, if we are available, we say yes to every invitation to hang out that they offer. We love spending time with them. During those times we relish our shared experiences, we talk about our hopes, dreams, and fears, and we cultivate a history together. Sure, it is wonderful to meet new friends and to explore their story and to get to hear what has happened in their life, like finding a new delicious food that has become your new favorite. However, there is nothing like having a friend you have known for a long time. Your relationship has stood the test of time and you have a multitude of shared experiences, stories, and inside jokes. Those friendships are like a favorite sweater that you know feels cozy and goes with everything—as soon as you put it on, you feel comfort. I want to have that kind of relationship with the Lord. I want to reminisce about our history of time spent together. I have a record of things He's said to me, how I have seen Him move in my life, and a love I have developed for Him. Those things can only come with time spent in His Presence. Determine that you want to spend more time with Him and then make the decision to actually do that. More on this to come in later chapters.

Falling in love: Spend time with Him in prayer.

Developing a life of prayer is much like getting to know your best friend better. You do this by talking with them and spending time with them. We can talk to Him as we would a friend, but we also need to let Him talk to us. This is not a one-sided relationship where we tell Him all the things we need Him to fix, and then leave our time together without giving Him time to reply. You know the kind of friend I am talking about. Most of us have had friends that monopolize the conversation and tell you everything about their day and life, but never take a breath to ask about what is going on with you. I've had a friend or two like that. In the olden days when phones had cords, and there was only one or maybe two of them in the house, I would sit by the phone to "talk" to my friend. The only thing is, I would not talk but listen. Five minutes would go by and I had not spoken a word. I remember my mother saying that it was a one-sided conversation. I was never asked about what was going on in my life, but I knew what was happening in my friend's life in minute detail. I don't want my relationship with the Lord to be like that, one-sided. I want to give time and space for hearing what He is saying back to me. I am not just throwing out there all my worries and anxieties in the form of "prayer requests," but I am cultivating a relationship with the One who is so madly in love with me and knows every fiber of my being, for He lovingly and purposefully created me.

Falling in love: Consume His Words on a daily basis.

The Scriptures are His love letter to us, about us, and for us. Reading the Word of God is like looking at photographs of someone's family and friends, of vacations they took, of milestones they reached. Those pages contain the unfolding story of God's love for humanity, and of humanity's reaction to Him. It contains mysteries that beg to be unlocked, and of the shockingly raw and unfiltered passion the God of the Universe has for His children. The Word of God brings us life and hope. It is like consuming a spiritual smoothie each day which allows us to be able to walk through each day with stamina, courage, and expectation.

The Lord invites us to come and dine on His Word. He wants us to "taste and see that [He] is good" (Psalm 34:8 NLT). He has prepared a feast for us to partake of through His Word, and yet so often we want to just go through the drive-through at McDonalds and just get the fast food version. Read His Word. Spend the time savoring every morsel of it in your mouth like a gourmet meal; don't be in such a hurry to read a verse on the go like a quick snack. There is buried treasure in His Word that He delights in revealing to us.

Think of this: I love the smell of fresh bread being baked. I can smell that smell, but unless I actually eat the bread, it is not satisfying to me. He has prepared dishes and foods for us which we know not of; there are depths of revelation in Him, and depths of His love, and depths of experience in Him we have not tasted. It is His heart for His bride to dine with Him. There are depths and chasms and crevices and Grand Canyons of His character and personality we have not yet discovered which only come from cultivating a relationship with Him. For all eternity we will spend eons mining the different facets of the many diamond-like sides of the characteristics and meanings of all His Names, His Ways, His Words.

Read His Word and dig out the nuggets of gold in the Word like you are mining for diamonds. Bible Teacher and International House of Prayer founder, Mike Bickle, says, "The Holy Spirit through the Word escorts us on this Divine Treasure hunt into the beauty of Jesus." The Word is a treasure hunt, a road map into every reflection and crevice of the Savior's face. There are treasures to be excavated out of it, treasures which will make you wealthy in spirit.

> "Oh the depth of the riches both of the wisdom and knowledge of God! How unreachable are His judgments and unfathomable His ways! For who has known the mind of the Lord or who became His counselor? Or who has first given to Him that it might be paid back to Him again? For from Him and through Him and to Him are all things. To Him be the glory forever."
> (Romans 11:33-36 NASB)

It is one thing for someone else to dig out a jewel and give it to you, it is another thing for you to find it for yourself. It is wonderful to enjoy someone else's revelation of the Word, but don't let that be the only way you learn about Him. Allow Holy Spirit to reveal to you a priceless personal revelation through His Word which is just for you. It is alright to eat someone else's revelation, but there comes a time in your walk with the Lord He wants you to eat for yourself. Just like when I would feed my children a bottle, then from a spoon, then finger food they could pick up and put in their mouths. Eventually they graduated to eating meals at the table with the family and could sit on their own, no longer in the confines of a high chair. Eating someone else's revelation of the Word is great and those are awesome snacks, but He wants you to receive His manna for yourself.

You hold a treasure chest of jewels in your hands when you hold the Word of God, and yet so many are content to keep the lid closed. We often need help discovering what the Bible is trying to say to us. Holy Spirit is your teacher, and He loves to do what He does best—reveal Jesus. Invite Holy Spirit to read the Scriptures with you. Sit in His classroom and allow Him to teach you things that make your heart go pitter patter and your head spin.

Falling in love: Dedicate time for Him.

I felt that my relationship with the Lord was greatly accelerated when I started to set a time aside each day to get to know Him better. It was in those times I fell in love with Him. So how do we cultivate a daily time of meeting with the Lord? What do we do during that time?

Firstly, have a consistent place where you can meet and hang out with God. I have a comfy chair in my bedroom where I commune with the Lord. I have friends who have their quiet time with the Lord during their morning run, or in their car on their commute to school or work. Some have a prayer room, some sit at the kitchen table, or at a laptop, but the point is, make a daily appointment with the Lord and then have a consistent place where you meet with Him. This might change depending on what you have going on in your life. In some seasons of life, my meeting place of choice was a big comfy "prayer chair" that I could curl up into. I had all my resources and journals in a basket next to the chair. I would even get antsy if someone else tried to sit in my prayer chair! When my children were little, there seemed to be no place I could "get away" and I ended up fixing up part of my walk-in closet to be a refuge for my quiet time with God. During another time we lived a different house, the bathroom was my quiet space, probably because I could lock the door to ensure privacy! The actual place you meet with Him is not important, but the important thing is to set time aside to meet with Him and stick to it. If you made a date with a friend to meet them for dinner at a certain time and place, you'd make sure you were there. How many dates have we missed with God? The consistent place is not for His benefit; He is omnipresent and omniscient. But you aren't and discipline-wise it's easier to have a consistent place. It helps you get into a routine, helps your mind settle down and keeps your heart expectant to meet with Him.

Secondly, get a good study bible with a clear translation. I have a bible called the Hebrew-Greek Key Study Bible which allows me to look up words in Hebrew and Greek at the back of the bible. It really brings the Scriptures alive for me. I also sometimes use my journaling bible, which allows me to draw, color and doodle in the wide margins my thoughts as I read. The Passion Translation is a new favorite translation of mine. The Scriptures come alive in beautiful ways in this translation. It is helpful to have a few translations you can read the same verse from. Some would rather use a Bible phone app, and that is great if it works for you. Just be wary that your phone is not a place set apart for God, as anyone or anything may ding in with a notification, breaking into your set-apart time and space. (Some apps have a setting to prevent this!) I personally love to hold the Bible in my hands, to write in the margins, highlight verses, and mark down dates a particular verse really spoke to me. I have also discovered a new app called Dwell, which is a spoken bible app. To have the Word of God spoken to me with beautiful accented voices and soft music I can choose in the background is very soothing. Whatever works best for you—figure out what that is, and get what you need to have the Word available in the best format for you.

Thirdly, have a "tool box," containing a bible concordance, commentaries, bible dictionary, bible history, and general bible information (or phone apps that can provide you those!). Arm yourself with whatever you need to make searching the scriptures easier for you. I like www.blueletterbible, and www.esword. There are lots of apps and web sites for you to choose from. The point is, open that treasure chest and let the love letters the Lord has written to and for you pour out. Absorb them, devour them, digest them and then activate the power that the Word brings in your life.

How can you structure your daily quiet time with the Lord?

Through trial and error over the years I have known the Lord, I want to share with you what has worked for me. I have usually found it difficult to concentrate. Can I get an "Amen!"? I'd sit down to have a time with the Lord and I could not quiet myself enough to concentrate on Him, but would think the most random of thoughts. Did I ever text that friend back? Did I DVR my favorite upcoming TV show? I really need a cookie . . . The list goes on. I found that I almost needed to train my brain in order to connect with Him. Here's what I did and it worked! I got this idea from a book I read by Becky Tirabassi. I took a notebook and sectioned off with dividers and labelled them: Worship, Admit, Requests, Thanks, Listening, Bible Journaling. I would start with the worship section and would literally write out the lyrics to worship songs that really touched me or I connected with. I would go over the words and sing them back to the Lord, or pray the lyrics back to Him. I found I would connect with the Lord in this way and my thoughts would quiet down as I concentrated on Him and His goodness. Some days, I would play worship music, mulling over the lyrics and connecting with the Lord. Other days I had no words and would lay on the floor and play worship music and think about Him. This way I would soak in His Presence and my thoughts would be turned to Him.

Next, I would ask the Lord what grieved Him; anything I had done, or said or thought that day. I would repent of those things which had taken me out of alignment with Him and then I would receive His forgiveness. I needed to learn to then let those sins go—because He does—rather than bashing myself with feelings that I was bad or would never measure up. That being said, I rarely would write down what I was repenting of. When the Lord forgives, He erases our sins and removes them from us so I wouldn't need to record those things and then not need to reread it. I would wait on Him until I found I was not hearing anything else to repent of. I also started taking communion during that time when I felt led. I have experienced some beautiful times of connection with the Lord when I take communion privately with Him.

Then I would turn to the requests section and there I would write down the things that I was praying for: friends, family, life events, direction, etc. I would write the date I started praying for those things, and then the date the request would be answered. Sometimes they were not answered the way I thought they would be, but they were answered none the less! It is so fun to go back years later (yes, I've kept my journals that long) to look at what I had prayed for and how those prayers have been answered. It is very encouraging to see. Some of the things that had consumed my worries I could look in hindsight and realize the Lord's bigger plan was so much better that the obstacles I couldn't see beyond.

The next section I'd turn to is thanks. What a great habit to get in to, giving thanks. I would thank the Lord for small and big ways in my life He made a difference, I'd thank Him for answers to requests and for how He deemed to answer them. The more I thanked Him, the more my attitude changed from worried and frazzled to grateful and peaceful. There are some great books that confirm this. Ann Voskamp's One Thousand Gifts is filled with how-tos on cultivating a lifestyle of thankfulness.

I would then turn to the listening section. This is where I would get quiet before the Lord and listen to what He put on my heart and that is what I'd record. Some days I'd have a lot to write and other days I wouldn't hear anything. That is ok! The requests section time was when I did most of the talking, but the listening section reminded me to get quiet and let Him speak to me.

I'd end with the bible journaling section. This is where I'd read a verse, or a passage or chapter and write down my reflections on it. A lot of times, I would write questions about the passage and that gave me a good springboard to ask the Lord for clarification or I would study it out with the resources I had. Before I knew it, I would easily fill up 20 minutes, 30 minutes, and even an hour of time spent with the Lord! I found that the structure really helped me and I continued that for years. Now I have a more relaxed way of meeting with the Lord because it has become easy for me to hear His voice and let Him lead our time together. Please don't wait until you feel you have gotten your act together to set aside time to meet with Him. Start now.

You are cultivating a relationship with the Creator of the Universe and He wants to spend time with you! I found that getting myself into a schedule of meeting with Him really helped me. The seasons of our life ebb and flow, and during certain times you may be able to spend gobs of time with God; but in other seasons you are so busy so it is challenging to set time aside. I would allow my God-time to be incorporated into my schedule for each season of life. I remember when I was first getting serious about cultivating my God-time, I would literally write the

> *There is no right or wrong way to meet with Him. Just meet!*

appointment with God and the time I wanted to do it in my calendar. This helped keep me motivated and accountable, at least most days. I often felt like I was so busy, I did not have time to spend with Him; however, when I contemplated how much screen time I spent each day, or time watching movies, shows, or hanging out with friends, I decided that I really did have time to spend with Him. Regardless of what time, where you meet, or how you structure your quiet time, incorporate a space into your day so you can develop a lifestyle of friendship with the Lord. Everyone's quiet time with the Lord will look as individual as they are. Remember, there is no right or wrong way to meet with Him, just meet!

I will probably never create an Instagram account of my shared experiences, joys, and history with the Lord; but, if I did, I hope it would contain post after post of exciting encounters, memories of time spent together during tough, hard times, happy, joy-filled times, and of course beautiful photography in His stunning creation. I want to know Him. I want to have a lifetime of love that I can tell others about. My love story with the Lord is continuing to grow and develop. This pursuit of getting to know the Lord on a deep and meaningful level is not easy; it is a commitment. However, I am on a journey and each step is allowing me to fall deeper and deeper in love with Him. This is the journey of a Warrior Princess. And it is your journey, too.

Prayer:

Lord, it is my desire to fall in love with You. Give me the longing to want to take those steps to develop a daily quiet time where I can learn more about You, and fall in love with You. Help me to incorporate time with You into each day. I am walking deeper into Your heart as You open my eyes and ears to hear and see You more clearly. Activate my Spirit to reach out to you during my days so that I can connect with You as I would with a dear friend. Help me to love You well. Amen.

Activation:

Dream with the Lord what your ideal meeting time with Him would look like. On a piece of paper, write down what your quiet time might look like. Think of those home makeover shows. This is your "Great Quiet Time Makeover." Ask the Lord, "How do You want to design my quiet time with You?" Think of a place you'd like to consistently meet, and a time that would work for your schedule. Be willing to be flexible if that time doesn't work, but take steps towards making that a reality in your life. Write down your commitment to the Lord of meeting with Him and write it in your iPhone or calendar. Take that step of getting to know Him in a deeper way. It is the best investment you will ever make!

Huddle Questions:

1. What are the struggles you've had in the past with trying to develop and commit to a daily quiet time with the Lord?

2. The title of this session is "Falling in Love with Jesus." What are your thoughts on that?

3. Share what you would ideally like your quiet time to look like.

4. In Dana Candler's book *Entirety*, she writes, "How often the Lord is loved partially without being loved *unrestrainedly*. Yet what would it look like if there were a people, a generation that burned in a fervency of love marked by a radical resolve to love Him in the way that He Himself loves—without restraint?" What are your thoughts on this quote?

Girls with Gumption: Corrie Ten Boom

I have never kept a secret which helped save someone's life, but Corrie Ten Boom did. Corrie was born in Amsterdam in 1892. She and her sister, Betsy, worked in their father's watch shop and Corrie became the first female watchmaker licensed in Holland. The close family of 6 lived above the watch shop and loved hosting, feeding, and caring for others in need. During the war World War II, Nazi soldiers were capturing people of Jewish descent and sending them to Hitler's concentration camps where eventually six million would be killed. The Ten Boom family hid and saved hundreds of Jewish people during the war in Corrie's bedroom, which was fitted with a secret hiding place. Behind a concealed door, six people could be hidden from Nazi soldiers when they would search the Ten Boom house. Sadly, after being tipped off by an informant posing as someone needing help, Nazi soldiers captured the Ten Boom family and sent them to separate concentration camps. During her time there, Corrie held on to her faith in the Lord and prayed she would be able to be reunited with her beloved sister Betsy. The Lord answered her prayer and Corrie was sent to the same camp as Betsy. Together the heroic sisters held bible studies and encouraged the other prisoners. Sadly, Betsy died while imprisoned, but miraculously, Corrie was released on a technicality a few days later.

Corrie became an effective evangelist, went on to write numerous books about her captivity and was able to forgive her captors, one of which even attended a speech Corrie was giving in America years later. She did not hold on to unforgiveness or the lies which came with her trauma, but released them to the Lord and allowed His Truth to heal her. Her sunny attitude inspired many to not allow their circumstances or traumas to define them. This Warrior Princess' faith and bravery encouraged many in the midst of terrifying and tragic circumstances.

3

How to Catch An Arrow

"God takes our sins—the past, present, and future, and dumps them in the sea and puts up a sign that says NO FISHING ALLOWED."

– Corrie Ten Boom

The other day a friend was telling me how they felt like they had been slapped across the face by someone. They did not mean they were physically slapped, but instead cutting words were the weapon of choice. Have you ever been on the receiving end of words that sting, words make you feel shame, words that cause you to question if you can do anything correct? Often traumatic circumstances and explosive encounters can turn into toxic lies that we come to believe about ourselves.

Corrie Ten Boom understood the slap of stinging words, as well as the physical torment of imprisonment in Nazi concentration camps in World War II. Corrie Ten Boom's story could have caused her to be forever held in a real prison, and in a prison of her own making. However, it was her belief that the Lord wanted her to live a life serving Him and to serve others. Corrie writes her prayer was, "Lord Jesus, I offer myself for Your people. In any way. Any place. Any time."[3] The Lord took her up on that prayer.

Corrie refused to let her circumstances define and identify her. She did not allow her story's injustices and tragedies become a filter through which she viewed everything. Clearly, it was a freeing and redemptive power in her life. But how do we keep the painful experiences from changing our outlook?

I read the following quote on a sign the other day: "Life is not about waiting for the storm to pass, but it is about learning to dance in the rain."[4] It struck a chord deep in me; I just can't forget it. How many times have I allowed discontentment and restlessness to creep into a day where things do not go as planned? It ruins my perception of myself and everything around me. I want to learn to dance in the rain!

Have you ever considered that life might be like one big dance? Our life may have cringe-worthy moments, like when the guy we don't like asks us to dance, or moments of standing alone watching other couples at dances. Our dance could also include moments of joining in a big circle and dancing your heart out with friends. Like middle or high school dances, we may dance with people who step on our toes, or who may judge us for how well we can or can't bust a move.

In the story of our life, the Lord asks us to dance. He invites us to step to the middle of the dance floor and allow us to be enveloped by His embrace. He is the perfect dance partner. He never judges what we are wearing, or if we are doing the steps just right. He asks us to dance with Him, but often times we cannot accept that invitation to dance, for many reasons.

Dance of the Arrows

I once heard a friend talk about how we sometimes dance with arrows embedded in our hearts. People try to get close to us, but cannot, because the imaginary arrow shafts prevent close proximity. That produced such a vivid picture, this dance of the arrows. A useful metaphor, I think. Let me elaborate . . .

Each trauma that we endure, each hurtful accusation, every painful interaction wounds us like an arrow piercing our heart. Historically, arrows were weapons of choice in war. While not powerful by themselves, arrows become a deadly projectile in the aimed bow of a warrior. Arrows were weapons meant to cause their recipients deep wounds, and even death. Sometimes, arrows were even dipped in poison to distribute venom through the bloodstream of its target, with the intent to kill the victim through poison if the piercing of the arrow did not kill them first. Just like real arrows, our heart and soul can be wounded in similar ways.

Often these imaginary arrows remain stuck in us for long periods of time and they can unfortunately shape who we are, and even reshape our identity. When someone tries to come close to ask us to dance, we can't accept with all the arrow shafts sticking out of our chest, preventing us from getting close. It is like imagining two porcupines trying to dance with one another. Their quills prevent them from getting close enough for a slow dance. What produces these arrows that we may have protruding from our hearts? Where do they come from? What do they look like? Well, here are a few loose typologies for these soul-wounding arrows.

The Arrow of Shame

I remember in grade school asking my teacher for help with a math problem I was struggling with. She was trying to help me, but I was having a hard time grasping the concept she was teaching. I approached her desk for the third time, because I still didn't understand. Obviously tired of my questions, she commented on my lack of understanding. I can't even remember what she said, but whatever it was made me feel like there was no use receiving any more help. The point was clear—I was hopeless at math and I had better not ask for any more help. I was humiliated in front of the whole class. I remember finding my way back to my seat, my face burning red. That incident left me feeling like I was not smart enough to understand math, and that arrow shaft was left embedded for years. I never pursued higher math outside of high school and my last math class I ever took was a vocational math class in 11th grade. It wasn't until years later I realized I was believing a lie, and I was actually good at conceptualizing math concepts (this was only discovered later when I was helping my own children with their math problems). But, because of that brief interaction—which I'm sure was never my teacher's intention—I came away feeling I would never be successful in math which shut down any further pursuit of the subject. That wrong belief changed the trajectory of my studies, that lie convinced me I was a failure, and that arrow of shame told me I

The arrow of shame convinces you that you are not good, that you are a disappoinment, that you are a failure.

was a disappointment.

In the story of my life, shame told me I wasn't good enough. I measured my ability by an unrealistic standard: sometimes it was manifested in comparison to others, but mostly just an unattainable level of expectation I placed on myself. Let's take a look at God's response to our shame.

After the bite of the apple in the Garden of Eden, Adam and Eve felt shame when sin entered, so they reached for fig leaves to cover themselves. Adam said to God, "I heard the sound of You in the garden, and I was afraid because I was naked; so I hid myself" (Genesis 3:10 NASB). Shame causes us to want to hide, telling us that we just do not measure up. The arrow of shame makes us feel like we have messed up somehow, and there is no hope so we might as well give up. Even perfectionism is a form of shame: We do not measure up and so we strive to make ourselves better, never quite reaching our unattainable standards. When Adam and Eve heard God's voice in the garden, they did not run towards Him and explain what had happened. They hid, filled with shame.

God does not want us to hide *from* Him, but run *to* Him. He wants to be there in the midst of our mess to help us sort it out. We have a place at His Table. He doesn't remove our place setting because we messed up; quite the opposite. Being part of His family means working through our setbacks and figuring out our identity—not based on our failures, but on who our Father says we are. We may not be perfect, but Father God is, and He wants to help us see who we really are: a daughter of the Most-High God, the God who sees us in our brokenness and loves us back to wholeness through His extravagant love. Shame causes us to hide, but Isaiah 61:10 (NASB) tells us He has clothed you with garments of salvation and wrapped you in a robe of righteousness. Remember this! He loves you, just the way you are.

The Arrow of Fear

A friend of mine with five children went to Costco to get groceries for the week. There were long lines, complaining kids, tears, snacks doled out, and even one temper tantrum. She managed to get all the groceries and kids in the van and off she went. She had just caught her breath when she heard a small voice from the back row ask where her oldest child was. She had left a child behind! The child left at Costco ran a gamut of emotions. They had been

distracted looking at the
books while the family had
gone ahead to the checkout
line. When the child went
to look for the family and

> *The arrow of fear convinces you
> that you are alone.*

didn't see them, mild panic turned into full blown fear. This child
was all alone in a busy store full of people. The arrow of fear told
them that they were all alone.

Like the child left at Costco, have you ever looked around a
crowded room and felt all alone? It is interesting that in God's love
letter to us, He mentions "do not fear" over 300 times! We are the
opposite of alone, for He tells us He will never leave us or forsake us.

I used to be afraid of the dark, but then realized that really I
was afraid of being alone in the dark. Similarly, I remember when
my daughter as a little girl, she, too, was afraid of the dark and had
a hard time falling asleep. So at bedtime I would sit in a chair in her
room. Every night, our routine would go like this:

"Mom?"

"Yes, sweetie? What is it?"

"Nothing, just want to make sure you're still there."

How comforting it was for her to just know I was there. Even
greater comfort comes from knowing that God is there for us. He is
there and will be there for you, always. Next time you feel that arrow
of fear pushing itself into your heart, remind yourself that there is
a "fear not" voiced by the Lord for every situation you encounter,
and every trauma you have and ever will walk through. Fear may tell
us we are all alone but He says to us, "Be strong and courageous!
Do not tremble or be dismayed, for the Lord your God is with you
wherever you go" (Joshua 1:9 NASB).

The Arrow of Rejection

My dear friend, Shelby, had high hopes she would be asked
to prom by the boy from science class that she was developing a
relationship with over text. They would see one another in the halls
at school and in class, but it would be through their phones that they
could express how they were feeling. She picked out a prom dress
and planned with her friends where they would take pictures and go
for dinner. The next day at school, in a sea of students she spotted
her guy with a sign in his hand. "This is it," she thought, "He's

going to ask me to prom!" She hurried over to where he was standing and the crowd parted to reveal he was embracing another girl and handing her flowers. She was not the one he wanted to ask; he had

> *The arrow of rejection convinces you that you are not good enough, that you are not wanted.*

asked someone else. The arrow of rejection embedded itself into this sweet girl and she ended up not even going to prom. The arrow of rejection told her she was not good enough.

The arrow of rejection tells us we are not wanted, but the Lord tells us we are accepted. If you have ever felt rejection then you have been subjected to a conditional love that says "If I feel you are worth it, then you will receive my love." You may have sadly felt this from parents, coaches, boyfriends, and friends. This lie becomes embedded in us and we begin to believe we walk through life constantly not accepted by others. This filter clouds our ability to meet new people and tackle new things, because we begin to think others will not want us around. With this arrow embedded deep in us, it seems we suddenly know what everyone is thinking! We suspect that those around us think we are lesser, unworthy, unwanted. We remove ourselves from friends, and do not experience that fulfillment of belonging to a community. We wither away in our rejection. We put ourselves in isolation and refuse to let others get close to us, or reject them before they can reject us. Can you see how this arrow can wreck our relationships with others and with God?

If the arrow of rejection is embedded in our heart, when we sin and mess up we feel we need a self-prescribed time out in order to sufficiently punish ourselves. What's worse, is after our self-prescribed punishment, we think we might as well not try to get close to Him again because He will not accept us. People who feel the arrow of rejection may manifest that lie through cutting, food disorders, or other self-harm, or even something as seemingly harmless as isolation by being emotionally distant. In each manifestation, we may believe that God could never accept us. However, that is the anatomy of a lie—it tells us the opposite of what truth tells us. The truth is that Jesus came and died just for you! He takes your face in His hands and says "You belong to Me." He tells us in Ephesians 1:6 (AMP) that you are accepted in the Beloved. Yes *you*, not the person behind or beside you, but *you*! Jesus felt your rejection that you may think no one else can know the sting of. He was well acquainted by the torment of rejection and was despised and rejected of men who hid their faces from Him (Isaiah 53:3 NLT). Fear may tell us we are not accepted, but Jesus comes in the midst of your rejection to tell you that you are His.

The Arrow of Worthlessness

The arrow of worthlessness tells us we are unlovable or bad. This is highlighted and exacerbated by social media where people can often post anonymously about others, nastiness that would probably never be said to their face. Behind the anonymous covering of a computer, cyber bullies exude a false sense of security and heightened bravado. We have heard of people shutting down their social media accounts after rude and hurtful comments are made public for all to see. Suicide has even been the result of such situations. The arrow of worthlessness leaves us isolated and feeling like we will never be loved.

> *The arrow of worthlessness convinces you that you do not measure up, that you have no value.*

The arrow of worthlessness tells us that we do not measure up and have no value to ourselves, others and to the Lord. Life circumstances may have told us we are unloved, or loved less than the next person. This is highlighted when we scroll through social media and see how everyone else must have a fabulous life, tons of friends, a boyfriend that adores them, and are super successful in everything they want to do. Social media can often make us feel so ordinary. We are not sipping umbrella drinks by the pool showcasing our perfect pedicure, or laughing with abandon, arms slung around myriads of friends at a concert. But in real life, who is? If we live with the arrow of worthlessness, we are always thinking someone else has it better than us. Someone else is always "more" than you (more beautiful, more successful, more clever, more loved . . .). The fact is though, there will always be someone that we can envy. But that is just not how we are called to walk through life; always feeling second-place to someone else. Thankfully, God does not always use those that are the prettiest, or most gifted, or have it seemingly all together, but He uses those in whom His character is developed.

Worthlessness makes us feel we can never work hard enough or do enough to win others approval. This sets us up on an exhausting hamster wheel of striving to be what we think everyone wants us to be, do, or say to gain their love and approval. Do you know what though? God is not comparing us to anyone else! He tells us in Psalm 139:17-18 (TPT) that every single moment He is thinking of us. How precious and wonderful to consider He cherishes us and we are constantly in His every thought. His desire for us is more than the grains of sand on every shore! Even when we wake up in the morning, He is still with us! This is not a God who has a measuring stick out to see if we have measured up that day. *No.* This is God, who is so overwhelmingly in love with us that He can't take His mind, or His eye, off of us! This is a God who can't wait until you wake up in the morning so He can start the day with you. You are worth it. He made you! Psalm 139:15-16 (TPT) says, "You even formed every bone in my body when You created me . . . You saw who you created me to be before I became me! Before I'd ever seen the light of day, the number of days you planned for me were already recorded in Your book." You are His exquisite creation. Your worth and value are contained in that truth.

The Arrow of Insecurity

When she was younger, my daughter experienced bullying by one of the girls in her class. This left her feeling insecure and wary of friendships. Another friend invited her over and in the privacy of the friend's room, asked my daughter about her experience with the bully. My daughter gave an honest report of what the bully had said to her and how that made her feel. There was a snickering sound coming from the closet, and after some rustling around, the bully stepped triumphantly out of the closet. My daughter was horrified that the bully had again pulled one over on her, and disappointed that the other "friend" was in on the joke. She ran from the room crying. That arrow of insecurity told her that she was not safe, and that she was unprotected. It took a while for her to trust friends again.

> *The arrow of insecurity convinces you that you are not safe.*

The arrow of insecurity tells us that we are not safe, but rather vulnerable and powerless. This can cause us to try to control everything by building walls of self-protection so others cannot hurt us further. That might sound dramatic or silly, but that is indeed what we do when met with insecurity, on some level or another. Fear and anxiety become our friends as we try to protect ourselves from perceived dangers, real and imagined. Sometimes we try to comfort ourselves with food, binge-watching, shopping, etc. This just builds up higher walls of addiction, compulsive behaviors, and indifference. Sometimes the arrow of insecurity causes us to be impulsive: "That top is such a good price, I don't want to miss out on such a great deal." We try to make ourselves feel safe and secure by amassing "things" around us, but that does not fill us up. The dictionary definition for secure means to feel safe, stable, free from anxiety and fear, or to not have a care. Free from anxiety and fear? May sound like a long shot. Take heart, however! The angel of the Lord encamps around those who fear Him and rescues them (Psalm 34:7 NASB). Could it be we can truly only feel secure when we are hidden in Him? God tells us that we can be safe and confident in His love. Psalm 5:12 (NASB) tells us that He surrounds us with favor as with a shield. We are secure in His abounding love.

Dealing with Your Arrows

You can see how it is so easy to allow these arrows to torment us when we experience traumatic circumstances, but sometimes it can just be the cares of life and rubbing up against mean people, or our incorrect responses to those things. These arrows sneak into our lives and remain embedded in our hearts, fueling the lies that we begin to believe about ourselves.

The Lord comes to us and He asks, "Will you dance with Me?," and we do the dance of the arrows. "I don't know the steps," we say. "I don't know how to dance with the arrows sticking out of my heart." "It is too painful to dance." Any number of excuses . . . Through our experiences, we may have learned not to trust others— and we may conclude that we cannot even trust God.

Each trauma I experienced, each word-curse that was aimed at me, was like an arrow pressed into my heart. The Lord would ask me to dance with Him and I couldn't get close enough to Him to dance. I looked at the Lord through the filter of lies. "You're not good enough" the arrow lied to me, so I couldn't get close to the Lord. Other people in my life would ask me to dance and my arrows prevented me from getting close to them or from them getting close to me. I began to live life out of my belief system composed of lies about myself. That belief system acts as a filter through which I viewed relationships, the world, and God.

What if we were able to identify those arrows for the lies they are? What if we were able to capture those arrows before they ever became embedded in our heart? It is possible, I assure you, both in the natural world and the spiritual.

Imagine a Warrior Princess, hair flowing and horse sweating, as she rides into battle. Arrows whiz by her ear as she puts her head down, eyes forward as she steadies her hand on the horse's reins. She sees an arrow from a far off, its trajectory coming straight for her. Confidently she raises her arm, cups her hand in anticipation and snatches the arrow just before it pierces her heart. She cannot afford to have any arrow delay her from reaching her destiny. She determines no arrow will cause her to be entangled. No arrow may wound her. No arrow can slow her down from her destiny and where she is going.

"That's just fantasy!" you may say. Oh, really? Joe Alexander from Germany set a Guinness Book of World Records by catching 43 arrows by hand in two minutes. Wow! What if we rose to the call of our inner Warrior Princess to reach up and catch those arrows before they even had the chance to get close enough to become embedded in our hearts? What if then we took that lie-arrow, broke it in half and gave the broken pieces to Jesus? If I had known and understood that image so many years ago, I feel that I would have not suffered the anxiety and angst moving through life with arrows embedded in my heart. They affected my relationships, the way I saw myself, how I interacted with the world around me, and mostly how I viewed and received God's love.

So how do we get rid of these arrows and allow the Lord and others to come closer to us?

Dealing with Arrows: Ask Holy Spirit to reveal the arrows in your life

My friend, Cassie, had a series of questionable boyfriends, each more demanding than the next. She felt she could never measure up, or be good enough, or look pretty enough for them to want to stay with her. Finally, an amazing boy walked into her life! Though they started an incredible dating relationship, she broke it off as they started to care more deeply for one another. As Cassie reflected on it, she realized that she had rejected her ideal boyfriend, before he could reject her. She was living with the arrow of rejection, deepened by her previous break ups.

Being aware of how the circumstances we have walked through can affect us gives us insight into what lie-arrows we have accumulated in our hearts. If we are encountering constant rejection, or find ourselves saying, "this always happens to me," that could be the same lie that embeds itself in us over and over.

When you are in a situation and you feel you are going down the same path and reacting the same way you have before, it could be as a result of an arrow. Change your strategy. Ask Holy Spirit to reveal the lies that are embedded in your heart, preventing you from being free from those strongholds.

Dealing with Arrows: Catch the arrows before they land in your heart

Cassie was able to realize the arrow of rejection had clouded her vision and prevented her from fully engaging with the boyfriend she broke up with. Next time she met someone special, she was able to identify when the arrow of rejection tried to compromise her feelings of security, and she caught the arrow before it landed in her heart. She is now happily engaged to her current boyfriend.

Once you have identified the arrows you've dealt with in the past, you are aware of what those arrows feel like. You can then spot that lie coming towards you a mile away. The only reason we can capture the arrow and break agreement with that lie—break it in two—is because of the Truth in Christ. He alone is the One who whispers to us the Truth of Who He is and who we are. He is the light which shines in the dark place where those lies hide. His Word permeates with the Truth of who we are and Who He is. Only then can we discover our true identity as His Warrior Princess, free from every arrow.

Dealing with Arrows: Fill those wounds with truth from God's Word

The Word of God is the most powerful tool to heal the wound caused by an arrow. Hebrews 4:12 (TPT) says, "For we have the living Word of God, which is full of energy, and it pierces more sharply than a two-edged sword." It will even penetrate to the very core of our being, where soul and spirit, bone and marrow meet. It interprets and reveals the true thoughts and secret motives of our hearts.

Study His Word and ask Holy Spirit for promises which replace that lie. Whenever you receive a cut in the natural, you clean it and cover it to help it heal. We take the Water of the Word and clean out the wound where that arrow was, and allow the Truth of His Word to permeate the broken places and bring healing. When you accept the Truth, you begin the healing process.

If the arrow of shame says, "*You are not good enough,*" God whispers, "*You are Mine.*"

If the arrow of fear says, "*You are all alone,*" God whispers, "*I will never leave you.*"

If the arrow of rejection says, "*You do not belong,*" God whispers, "*You belong to Me.*"

If the arrow of worthlessness says, "*You are not as good,*" God whispers, "*There is no second place in Me.*"

If the arrow of insecurity says, "*You are not safe,*" God whispers, "*You are safe in My Presence.*"

> *His Truth brings healing. Allow His words to wash over you.*

When you learn how to catch the arrows, break them in two, and give them to Jesus, you have learned a strategy that will change your life, and change the way you will encounter every circumstance moving forward. You also learn a new dance-step. You no longer have a heart filled with arrows that prevent you from dancing with the Lord. You come into the intimate dance of communion with Him. You can receive the truths He whispers into our spirits. When you dance with the Lord, He looks at you and speaks the truth of who you are: you are wanted, you are chosen, you are clothed in righteousness, you are gifted, you are talented, you are sought after.

Those words of Truth break over us like a vial of perfumed oil and drip down covering every place of wounding where the arrows held us captive to their lies. The Truth He speaks over us brings healing, recalibration to the way we think, and strengthens and empowers us to face every new circumstance with new-found courage.

The Dance Ahead

I wish I could tell you that you will never meet another arrow, but the battle for your heart will rage on. There will still be lies in the form of arrows which barrel towards you as a result of circumstances you will encounter. That is just life. Bravely reach out and snatch those arrows! They will never be allowed to reach your heart. They are exposed for what they are—lies coming from the father of lies, our enemy.

I have heard that whatever you name, you have authority over, like Adam naming every animal in the Garden of Eden. Therefore, name every lie that assaults you, and expose it for what it is—not Truth.

As an example, try saying this: "To the lie of 'You are not enough,' we see you on the shaft of that arrow whizzing for our hearts after we have a day of failure and disappointment. We call you out, 'Not enough,' for the lie that you are; and, we refuse to give you a home in our heart. You have caused us pain and shame and embarrassment for the last time. We see you, we call you out for the destructive lie that you are, and we snatch you in our outstretched hand while all of Heaven cheers us on. We hold you high as you squirm in our grip, and we break you in half with a satisfying snap! We give the broken and useless weapon that you were into Jesus' outstretched, nail-scarred hand, and we cancel all agreement with you. We declare that we are more than enough in Him!"

What power in naming the lies that assault us! Give yourself permission to be honest with yourself as you begin to understand what arrows you may still carry. In this journey you reclaim your identity and step into a greater intimacy with God. The challenge is to experience His Truths in a revelatory way which allows a heart damaged by so many arrows to begin to be healed by the impact and ownership of His Truths. He, then, becomes the stronghold of Truth in our lives, not the arrows. Psalm 27:1 (NIV) says, "The Lord is my light and my salvation, whom shall I fear? The Lord is the stronghold of my life; of whom shall I be afraid?"

We need to know how to walk through the minefield of life and not get continuously wounded by the careless words and actions of others. That is not our inheritance. Jesus did not shed His Blood for us so we could walk around with arrows protruding out of our heart, afraid to fall down and press the arrow heads even deeper into our flesh. He died so that we could run unencumbered by all attacks of the enemy and free from the words and actions of other wounded people. I can't speak for you, but I don't want to continuously be tormented by rejection, or shame, or . . . the list goes on. I want to be victorious in every area of wounding, because I have learned how to identify those arrows aimed at me and have learned to catch those arrows before they become embedded in my heart.

He asks you to dance. Say yes and step close to Him, laying your head on His chest because there is nothing between you which prevents you. There is no arrow shaft, no festering wound, just you and Him. Even if storm clouds gather over you, you will be okay, for you have learned to dance in the rain.

Prayer:

Lord, you know how hard it has been for me to allow You to come close. I have so many arrows in my heart. I ask that You would help me identify the lies which are attached to those arrows so I could break agreement with them. Heal the wounds in my heart caused from the trauma of those arrows. I receive Your Truth which counteracts every lie that has permeated my heart. Infuse me with courage to reach up and capture those arrows before they can be embedded in my heart. I receive Your healing. Amen.

Activation:

You will need paper arrows precut for this activation. Also have a large trash can handy.

Invite Holy Spirit to highlight some of the arrows that have affected you. Quiet your heart and listen for His voice. Write down some of these false statements you have believed. Break agreement with those lies and physically tear the arrow in half and throw it away. Ask the Lord for the Truth from His Word which is an antidote to the lie. Declare His Truth out loud, receive that Truth, and allow His healing to heal where that arrow once was.

Huddle Questions:

1. How can these lies affect my daily life?

2. How can I tell others are affected by my arrows?

3. How can I keep the arrows from coming back to hurt me?

4. What do you think are the top 3 arrows young women deal with? Write them down and then write the corresponding truth the Lord would tell them.

Girls with Gumption: Kathryn Kuhlman

"I believe in miracles because I believe in God," was the catch phrase spoken in the lilting voice known at the time to thousands. People would come from all over to witness the miraculous healings which would take place at a Kathryn Kuhlman meeting. Empty wheelchairs would line the aisles, discarded by those who came in them but left walking and running on their own accord. At one point, Kathryn Kuhlman was one of the most famous and well known healing evangelists in the world. *"The St. Louis Globe Democrat Newspaper"* said that since 1948, two million had been healed by the power of God through Kathryn Kuhlman's ministry. Kathryn refused to be called a faith healer as she said it was God and Him alone who healed.

Kathryn Kuhlman was known for her special relationship with Holy Spirit and as she lovingly and reverently spoke of Him, people would experience healing right where they sat in her meetings. She was a woman who would hold captive people's attention as she listened to the inflections of God's voice. Kathryn was born in 1907 in Missouri. After an encounter with the Lord when she was 16, she started preaching and travelling with her sister and brother-in-law. Soon she encountered Holy Spirit, heard His voice and was never the same again.

In 1935 she founded the Denver Revival Center which grew to 2000 members. She started a Radio Show called *"Smiling Through,"* at a time when most people did not listen to a woman's voice; but, she later went on to have popular television shows which featured her sermons. The sick were brought to her meetings and tens of thousands left healed by the Lord. Kathryn always pointed others to Jesus. She would fill auditoriums to capacity (including Carnegie Hall), and would stop and listen for God's voice during the meeting to know what to do next.

She was sweet, flamboyant, and loved Jesus fiercely. This Warrior Princess started out hearing God's Voice for herself, but by the time she died in 1976, thousands had learned through her teachings to hear His Voice for themselves.

4

What Am I Listening To?

"I can't afford to have thoughts in my head about me that God doesn't have in His."

– Bill Johnson, Strengthen Yourself in the Lord

My friend went through the devastating loss of her house through a forest fire. Her neighborhood lost 346 homes. The morning of June 26, 2012, the smell of smoke hung in the air and tinted the sky an eerie yellow. At the time my friend called me late that afternoon, the fire raged at the end of her street. Through the cell phone, the fire sounded like a locomotive engine. "Just pray," she said somberly, and with that she and her husband got into their car and drove away from their house for the last time. When they returned days later, all that was left was smoldering ash.

In the midst of panic to evacuate, she had left her wedding ring on the counter. As I was praying for her, I heard the Lord say that she would find her ring again. "That's impossible," I thought. I texted my friend what the Lord had told me, too afraid to tell her face-to-face or by call what I had heard. *"Well, I did what you asked, Lord,"* I thought, but I didn't hold out much hope the ring would actually be found. About a week later, my friend called me crying, but this time it was happy tears! Incredibly, the ring had been found. Good friends had been sifting through the ashes, looking for anything that could be recovered, when the ring was uncovered. The setting was charred black, but the resilient diamond was intact and undamaged. The jeweler cried hearing her story when she brought the ring in to be re-set. It was a lesson to me to trust the voice of God.

God is always speaking to us. He speaks to us in many ways but the frequency of His voice is being broadcast loud and clear, 24 hours a day, 7 days a week. We are just often tuned in to the wrong station.

I'd like to think God's cell phone number is Jeremiah 33:3 (NASB), "Call on Me and I will answer you and tell you great and mighty things which you do not know." The word "call" in that verse means to cry out loud, to summon, to invite, and to roar. I love that picture of a roar—desperately crying out to Him to ask Him what He is thinking, what He wants to say to us.

Have you had someone call you on your phone from an unknown number and immediately launch into a tirade of what just happened to them? There are times I have no idea who just called and I strain to pick up clues from what they are talking about. How do I know this person? They obviously know me to launch into their conversation without a greeting. I have to wrack my brain and scroll down a list of possible people it could be and figure out who it is. I have had to stop someone before and sheepishly ask, "Ummm, who is this?" I don't know their voice well enough yet to be able to decipher who it is. I don't want this to happen with the Lord. I may not know the voice behind the unidentified number well enough, but I want to know His voice so well I do not have to ask Who it is. I do not want to ask the Lord when He is speaking to me, "Ummm, who is this?"

God speaks to His children (that is you!). Revelation 3:20 (TPT) says, "Behold, I'm standing at the door, knocking. If your heart is open

> God is always speaking to us.

to hear My voice and you open the door within, I will come in to you and feast with you, and you will feast with Me." The word "hear" in that verse is the Greek word akouo, which means to understand, and to hear with the ear of the mind. We cannot dispute often our real struggle is in our mind; the war which goes on between the voice of our flesh, the voice of God, and the voice of the enemy. In John 10:27 (TPT), He promises us that "My sheep hear My voice and

I know them and they follow Me." Did you catch that? He didn't say we should hear, or might hear, but He says we will hear. Period. It's a fact! There is no self-imposed time-out you can put yourself in which prevents you from hearing His voice. There is no amount of good works that catapults you to another ultra-Christian category that bestows supersonic hearing on you. You. Will. Hear. His. Voice. But what if you cannot decipher if it is His voice, your own, or something else?!

How can we recognize His voice?

There seems to sometimes be many voices in our heads. What you are hearing may be God's voice, your own flesh, or the voice of the enemy. We can learn to recognize a voice when you hear it. I've heard Bible teacher Joyce Meyer say "the battlefield is in the mind." That is so true. How many times have you been arguing with a voice in your head? Just like we can recognize the voice of a dear friend, we can learn to decipher God's voice, our voice, and the voice of the enemy. The enemy's voice is condemning and shaming. This voice uses fear to manipulate us and drive us. "You never get anything right! You say the stupidest things so shut your mouth! You are so worthless!" That is the enemy's voice attempting to derail us and stop us in our tracks. Sometimes our voice can sound similar to the enemy's. If we are still operating out of soul-wounds and lies, we may come into agreement with those strongholds and tell ourselves we can't do it, we will never be loved, we are not attractive enough ... You get the picture. The voice of God, however, gently leads us. It does not use fear to motivate us, but instead convicts us. His voice often feels like warm honey and makes us feel peaceful and centered. This is the voice I want to hear and be led by. Sometimes when I am listening for His Voice, I hear scriptures. The Lord draws from the well of His Word we have stored up in us by reading and meditating on the Bible. I have oftentimes felt like I did not understand the scripture passages I was reading and so have asked Holy Spirit to make it come alive and meaningful to me—and He has.

You get to know someone by spending time with them. Over time and shared experiences with them, you know the inflection, cadence, and tone of their voice. You can tell if they are happy or depressed just by listening carefully to their voice. Can we know God's voice this way? I can tell when someone from my family talks to me what they are feeling just by the tone of their voice. I can sense when they are discouraged by the cadence in their voice. I can tell when they are about to tell me good news by the way their voice goes up in inflection. I want to know God's voice like that. When one of my children says "Mom!," I can tell if they are mad, excited, or frustrated. Can we listen for God's voice that way? James 4:8 (NASB) says, "Draw near to God and He will draw near to you." He wants to personally talk to you. He wants you to clearly hear His voice. The Greek word for "draw near" is *eggizio* which means communion or to communicate. He is communicating with you. Are you listening?

How do YOU hear His voice?

In the perfectly-curated world of Instagram, it is difficult not to compare our lives with others.

I can't compare how I hear God's voice with how others hear. Many years ago, I was in a meeting where the teacher had us do some exercises which really freed me up from the lie that there is only one way to correctly hear His voice. She had us fold our hands together by interlacing our fingers. Is the left thumb on top, or the right thumb? There were people in the room who had the left thumb on top, and some who had the right. Which is the proper way? Exactly! Either is correct. Then she had us close our eyes and she said a series of words that we were to think about. She called out: mother, father, house, ice cream cone. We then opened our eyes and she asked us what we saw in our imaginations when she called out "mother." A majority saw a picture in their minds of their own mother, but some saw a drawing of a mother, some a cartoon image of a mother, some a woman but it was not their own mother. Fascinating. We went through all the words she had called out and discovered that not everyone in the room imagined the same thing. We are all unique, and how someone perceives an ice cream cone can be a black-and-white drawing or a full-color, three-scoop image of ice cream dripping down the cone. Which one is the most correct? All are! In the same way, people hear God's voice differently.

Some may hear His voice through a scripture they read or hear, some with the lyrics to a song, some through a message at church, or a podcast. I think you are getting the idea. God speaks to us in different ways and we need to be open to it and not judge how He speaks to someone else as better or not as powerfully as how you hear His voice. If you find He speaks to you mainly through His Word, then read away and let Holy Spirit open the Scriptures to you. If when you listen to worship songs or become lost in Him in a corporate worship time, write down what He is saying to you. If you receive revelation while listening to a podcast, talk to Him about it and journal. There is no "one way" to hear His voice. Discover how He mainly speaks to you and dive into that.

We can hear God's voice in so many ways. We can hear His voice through prayer. Prayer is having a conversation with God. Imagine Him sitting next to you. What do you want to say? Then get quiet and let Him respond. We've all had friends who monopolize the conversation and you can barely get a word in. You know everything about them and their day but they haven't asked you anything about yours. If prayer is a conversation with God then give Him time to respond to you. You may want to write it down. I often think I am going to remember everything He says but I don't. I go back to my journals and read them and remember what He has said. Sometimes it is more relevant to me the following week because of what I'm going through then.

We hear His Voice when we read His Word. Psalm 119:105 (NASB) says "Your Word is a lamp to my feet and a light to my path." I need that lamp and light when I am looking for direction and wisdom what to do.

When we have a difficult decisions or choice to make, we can hear His voice through our circumstances. Revelation 3:7.8 (TPT) talks about open doors and closed doors: "I've set before you a wide open door that none can shut." Sometimes we have a door of opportunity closed in our face. Rest in knowing that He opens and closes doors for us, and as we seek to know His will and listen to His voice, He responds.

Hearing the Voice of Holy Spirit

Holy Spirit also speaks to us. John 16:13 (NASB) says, "But when He, the Spirit of truth comes, He will guide you into all truth; for He will not speak on His own initiative, but whatever He hears, He will speak, and He will disclose to you what is to come." Jesus said He had to leave earth so Holy Spirit could come to teach us. I want to hear what Holy Spirit says!

He speaks to us through trusted counsellors, friends, and mentors. As I share my story with others and tell them I am asking for His voice to counsel me, they may have nuggets of truth I need to hear. If the Lord can speak to Balaam in the book of Numbers through his donkey, then He can certainly use our beloved friends and mentors to speak to us.

Another way Holy Spirit profoundly facilitates the Lord speaking to us is through His Word. Yet it is often hard to read His Word and receive revelation from it every time. It is easier to read the latest Christian book, listen to a podcast, or get insight from someone else's revelation instead of going directly to the Bible. Books and podcasts are great supplements to His Word, but should never take preeminence. Listening is active and requires mental effort and attention. Press in and ask Holy Spirit to illuminate the Scriptures for you so you can hear the Lord's voice in them. The more of God's Word inside of you, the easier it is to draw from that well of revelation.

Holy Spirit is also the Giver of peace, and this is an important way He speaks to us. Sometimes, when I am inquiring of Him, I have no peace in my spirit. I may be asking Him about a certain situation or something I need to decide about, and I feel no peace in my spirit to follow through with it. Other times, I may feel a real peace about taking a job, moving in with a roommate, or pursuing a relationship with someone. He gives us peace that transcends human understanding, and will make the answers known to you through Jesus Christ (Philippians 4:7 NIV). If I do not have peace about something, then I wait and do not move forward with that decision. He speaks to us in so many wonderful ways.

How to quiet other distracting voices

Our minds are like a theater that He speaks into, and we have a front row seat! Sometimes He speaks to us in pictures on the movie screen of our minds, sometimes in song, sometimes with words. There has never been a generation which has been so inundated with media and with the lure of destructive images, virtual peer pressure, and social-media din than this generation. We have to learn how our minds can remain sanctified and not defiled continuously by the images of this world. I believe one of the enemy's strategies to derailing this generation from their Kingdom purpose is through fantasy: pornography, erotic literature, movies, print media, and a fascination with the occult and horror genre. It is hard to keep our thoughts and minds pure in a culture which seeks to continuously keep it defiled. Even if you can keep your mind clean from such tarnish, the larger battle is just keeping it clear from the constant clutter and interruption of the information age.

When I think back to the exercise of calling out words and picturing them, it is much easier to picture what you know well. If

> *It is much easier to picture what you know well.*

you have a good relationship with your father, then you probably pictured him and not a drawing of a random man. And so it is with the Lord; if you know Him well, it is easier to picture, understand His thoughts, and hear what He is telling you. He created us and knows us so intimately that He knows how we are going to best hear His voice. So in a world where our minds may be very much cluttered with so many things, how can we clearly hear His Voice?

When I want to settle down and press in to hearing what He has to say to me, I often start with binding the voice of the enemy. For example, I may say "In the Name of Jesus, I bind the voice of the enemy. I want to only hear You speak to me Lord." When I start to pray, often my mind wanders and I think of all the things I have to do, who I was supposed to text back, what I have on my plate for the next week. There are so many portals now of communication: our phone, the many different outlets of social media (Instagram, Snapchat, Facebook, WhatsApp, etc.), and our computer, just for a start. That is a lot of voices vying for our attention as we try to listen for the one Voice we truly want to hear! I submit my thoughts to the Lord and ask Him to direct them. God's voice is often the One you hear right after you've asked Him a question, and right before you've begun to rationalize if that is really His Voice! Proverbs 3:5-6 (NASB) says, "Trust in the Lord with all your heart, and do not lean on your own understanding." The Hebrew word for trust in that verse translates to "attach oneself to." I ask to hear His voice, then I trust that He will respond to me. I attach myself to His voice. I can reason my way out of anything, but there is a trust I need to exercise that He really does respond to me.

I find it helpful to turn off my own problems so I can concentrate on listening for His voice. Like static on the car radio, I want to be tuned into Him and not every other thought which is competing for my attention. Philippians 4:6 encourages us to worry about nothing and pray about everything. Sometimes, I have a lot to pray about! I imagine gathering up all my worries and putting them into a bag and then walking them to the foot of the cross and putting them down, then walking away. "Do not return to pick up the bag," I repeat to myself, "Do not return!" Listening to worship music as I pray often helps me to settle down and concentrate on Him.

When we ask to hear God's voice, we then have to be quiet to listen for it. We can't hear well if we're talking all the time. We need to limit our own talking. Just like the friend who tells us all about what is going on in their life without asking about us, so we want to also be quiet so we can listen to what the Lord wants to say to us.

Sometimes when I try to get quiet to listen to the Lord, all my thoughts start to swirl around like leaves on a blustery fall day. I like to imagine the wind is calmed and the leaves fall to the ground. I can peacefully now listen without the cacophony of thoughts whirling around me. The Carmelites, a Roman Catholic religious order, had a similar idea. They taught that our thoughts are like busy bees frantically buzzing around. We call the bees back to the hive where the chaos is stilled and we find rest in the hush. Always remember in Psalm 46:10 (NLT) He invites us to "Be still and know that I am God."

Trust that you hear Him

Often when I hear from the Lord, I think that I will remember exactly what He says to me, but I have found that is not the case. Write it down! I like to have a journal near me, and I put the date down and write down what He is saying to me. I have gone back years later to read what He said and have enjoying observing how He has encouraged me through different circumstances and relationships. At the time, I did not know what the ending of that circumstance would hold, but He did, and I can see how His words gave me the reassurance and confidence to walk through it.

Do you ever carry on an inner argument with yourself? Should I do this, or that? When I was learning to hear His voice, I would at first bask in what He said to me. Then I would turn around and argue with myself if that really was His voice, or just me telling myself what I wanted to hear. I remember hearing a story of a family friend who was ministering in the Canadian Arctic. The settlements were very far away from each other and roads were covered in snow so snowmobile was how they travelled. They had just visited one settlement and were on to the next when our friend noticed that the gas tank was almost on empty. They stopped on the frozen tundra and our friend heard God say to ask for more gas and to lay his hands on the gas tank and pray. Ok, I don't know about you but that may sound crazy, right?! Well that is exactly what he did, laid his hands on the gas tank and prayed for more. They arrived at the next settlement an hour later and the needle was at the exact same place. They had enough gas. Don't argue mentally with yourself when you hear God's voice. He is speaking to you.

Other ways to Hear His voice

Sometimes I wake up in the morning with lyrics to a song at the forefront of my thoughts. This has happened many times. The Lord speaks to us even while we sleep! Zephaniah 3:17 says, "The Lord your God is with you, He is mighty to save. He will take great delight in you, He will quiet you in His love, He will rejoice over you with singing" (NIV, BSB). When you wake up with the words to a song on your mind, listen to those words carefully for your spirit could have been singing them during the night, or the Lord could have been singing those words over you. He speaks to us even while we are asleep. That is probably the time we are finally at rest and not contending for attention from everything else; our spirits are attentive to what Heaven has to say to us.

You may experience dreams during the night which may be occasional or frequent. Pay attention to those dreams, for the Lord speaks to us through our dreams. In the Old Testament, He spoke through dreams to His people and that was an expected way of communication. Abraham, Jacob, Joseph, Samuel, Solomon, Daniel, Peter, and Paul all experienced communication from God through dreams. Job 33:15-16 says, "He speaks in dreams, in visions of the night, when deep sleep falls on people as they lie in their beds. He opens the ears of men and seals their instruction" (NLT, NASB). There are many wonderful Christian dream interpretation classes and books that can help decipher dream symbols and allow you to piece together what the Lord is saying to you.

What happens if you try these things and still cannot hear His voice?

Take a deep breath. Everything is going to be alright. You *will* hear His voice. He is not withholding from you. There is no sin so great that He manipulates your relationship by withholding Himself from you. Isaiah 1:18 (NASB) says, "Come now and let us reason together . . . though your sins are as scarlet, they will be white as snow; though they are red like crimson, they will be like wool." He wants to talk to you, to talk it through, to bring you back to right relationship so you can enjoy that communion with Him.

If we have heard His voice in the past and now we are experiencing a lull, it could be that He is quiet. Do not be afraid of silence. When my husband and I were dating, I felt like our conversation had to keep going. There could never be silence between us or a lull in the conversation, because that would mean we had nothing to say to each other or we had nothing in common. That was not correct thinking on my part, however. The deeper our relationship progressed, we could spend long periods of time just enjoying one another's presence. We could sit next to each other on a long car ride and not say anything, and life was ok! Peaceful, even! So it is with the Lord. Sometimes He wants us to just sit with Him, not ask Him for anything, but just enjoy His Presence. Psalm 23:2 (KJV) says that He makes us lie down in green pastures; He leads us beside still waters. Enjoy the green pastures and still waters when He wants us to sit with Him. It is like ballroom dancing when the man moves his hand slightly and his partner responds—we need to be in sync with what He is doing, and that comes with time spent in His Presence. If you press in to hear His voice and it is absent, go back over the checklist of how we hear His voice to make sure He isn't speaking in a way you are not used to. We need to remember that the Spirit of the Living God who raised Christ from the dead dwells in us (Romans 8:11 NLT).

Imagine you hold in your hands a beautifully embossed and ornate invitation. After you turn it over again to make sure it is addressed to you, you excitedly peel back the corner of the envelope. Who would take such care in sending you such an exquisite summons? You admire the elegant scroll work as you trace the letters of your name. Opening the envelope and releasing the invite from its confines, you read the script. Why, it is an invitation from the Lord Himself! He is inviting you to step into a new level of communion with Him. He is inviting you to deeper levels of understanding and crisp clarity to hearing His Voice in new and fresh ways, thus drawing you into a deeper level of intimacy with the Creator and Designer of the Stars. Do you desire to come into that level of face to face communication with Him? What will your response be? Only you can decide. I encourage you to listen for His voice and to press into Him. His voice is the most important, life changing, and profound one you will ever hear.

Prayer:

Lord, I know You speak to me but sometimes it is hard to hear You. Take away everything that prohibits me from clearly hearing Your voice. I want to tune in to the frequency of Your Voice so that it is so familiar to me. I desire to know the inflections and cadence of Your Voice, for Yours is the voice I want to follow. Help me to practice listening for the different ways You speak to me and open up our time together so that I can be assured of Your Voice. I love you, Lord. I am listening. Amen.

Activation:

I was taught this activation many years ago at a seminar. Its impact has been profound on me and I have since modified it and taught it with all age groups. May it bless you as it has me.

This activity involves the group listening to God and writing down what they hear. After the exercise is finished, the leader will give the words to one girl. The group leader prays before the meeting and asks the Lord to highlight one girl to be the recipient of those words during the meeting. The leader does not reveal the recipient until the very end, after everyone has written down what they hear from God.

The leader asks the girls to quiet themselves and concentrate on the Lord. Bind the voice of the enemy. Ask the Lord for an encouraging scripture, picture, song lyrics or word that is for someone else in the room. The girls will write it down on index cards that were previously handed out. It is helpful to have worship music softly playing in the background. After it looks like the girls have all written something down, reveal the girl who will receive the words. One by one have the girls read out loud the words of encouragement and then pass the card for the girl to keep. Have the girl who is receiving read her card aloud for herself. It is often so powerful to note that there is a theme to the words, and some of them may have received the same scripture or words. The Lord speaks to us! This activation can be done a few times, given the time allotment, and may be done in subsequent sessions so all the girls get a chance to be the receiver.

Huddle Questions:

In small groups have the girls take out their journals or hand out a piece of paper. For this group, we are going to ask the Lord "Friendship Questions for God." We are going to dial down and invite His peace to quiet our hearts.

Take a minute or so and just think about the Lord. Focus on Him, see Him in your mind, and know He is thinking of you right now. Know He is desiring to share with you what He is thinking.

Ask the Lord the following questions, listen and write down what He says. You may want to share at the end of your time together what He was saying, or keep it private.

1. Lord, what do you like about me? Why?

2. What do You see when You look at me?

3. If my heart is your home, what does that home look like?

4. Lord, I believe You are saying to me . . .

Girls with Gumption:
Aimee Semple McPherson

From a young age, Aimee could grab people's attention and hold it. When she was 24 in 1915, she gathered a crowd in Mount Forest, Ontario by standing on a chair in the middle of an intersection in town. Grabbing her chair, she told the crowd to follow her to a nearby church where she preached to a captive audience. This Canadian farm girl would become a renowned evangelist who would speak to millions over the course of her life. Her flair for the dramatic peppered her sermons which pointed people to the gospel of Hebrews 13:8 (NLT) that "Jesus Christ is the same yesterday, today, and forever." Holding both preaching and healing services, thousands would attend Aimee's meetings.

After travelling full time as an evangelist in the United States she settled in Los Angeles. In January of 1921, she held healing meetings in San Diego. Over 30,000 attended. In 1923, she built and dedicated the 5,300 seat Angelus Temple and established the International Church of the Foursquare Gospel. The church had a large platform area which could be raised or lowered by hydraulic pistons. This would become the stage for the dramatic illustrated sermons Aimee would become known for. Aimee's preaching was warm, inventive, creative, and welcoming, drawing a diverse audience which included many famous Hollywood actors. One of the Temple ministries fed and met the needs of thousands destitute people in Los Angeles. Another ministry, the Prayer Tower, had intercessors praying 24 hours a day, 7 days a week, for needs and requests which flooded in by the thousands.

Aimee's heart for evangelism led her to the darkest corners of the city to love people to Jesus. Ever the pioneer, Aimee became the first woman in America to have a radio broadcasting license and one of the first women ever to preach over the radio. She founded a bible college which trained thousands for ministry. To help put into perspective her incredible accomplishments, it wasn't until 1920 that women were allowed to vote nationally for the first time.

By the time she passed away in 1944 at the age of 54, Aimee had left a legacy of a lifetime of loving others to the Lord. The Foursquare denomination, Angelus Temple, and Life Pacific University are just some of the fruit which remain from this innovative preacher and social activist. Aimee Semple McPherson was an amazing Warrior Princess with a fierce love for her Savior who pioneered a movement bringing others closer to the Lord.

5

The Frequency, Sound, and Power of Our Words

"Words are containers for power; you choose what kind of power they carry."

– Joyce Meyers

There are some random memories from childhood that occasionally waft across my mind like a casual wind on a calm, still day. One such memory is of a Reader we used in our fourth-grade class. This was a book that had the musty smell of an object which lived in the school classroom for years and was handled by countless students who doodled on its pages, folded the corners, and scuffed the outside hardbound cover. I can still see the bold type of the title that asked the question, "What is the one thing that starts and stops wars?" I remembered thinking perhaps it was the latest weapon, or an incident one country had with another; but, after turning the page to view the answer I was startled by the white page with one thing written on it. It said "WORDS" in bold face type. Words were the one thing that could start and stop wars. It is funny this is burned into my fourth-grade memory bank as being a defining moment. I have never forgotten that statement. Words have power.

Our Creator God deemed words of such importance that He chose to birth the entire universe with one—well, maybe four—"Let there be light." And God *said*. He could have clapped His hands and "bang" the world materialized before Him; or, He could have twirled around and, out of a whirlwind of cosmic twinkle dust, the earth would have transpired. But no, He chose to create the entire universe and countless galaxies with His words.

> *"In the beginning God created the heavens and the earth. The earth was formless and void, and darkness was over the surface of the deep, and the Spirit of God was moving over the surface of the waters. Then God said, 'Let there be light'; and there was light."*
> *(Genesis 1:1–3 NASB)*

How did that cosmic encounter look when God spoke and the world was formed? Let's journey back to the beginning of the world and take a peek at what happened. Of course, I wasn't there, but I think it may have gone down something like this . . . In Genesis 1, verse 1 we see God forming matter—cosmic, nuclear, and such. Verse 2 says the earth was without form. Perhaps these particles vibrated with anticipation and excitement, ready to spring into action as soon as God spoke! Verse 3 says the Spirit of God was moving, hovering, and brooding over the face of the waters. Maybe Holy Spirit caused the particles to be held together with His vibrational hovering, and then the power of God's voice shaped and defined the matter into an explosion of light when He commanded, "Let there be Light." His Words are powerful! Psalm 33:6-9 (NIV) says, "By the word the Lord the Heavens were made, their starry host by the breath of His mouth . . . For He spoke, and it came to be; He commanded, and it stood firm."

John 1:1 (NIV) tells us, "In the beginning was the Word, and the Word was with God and the Word was God." The Word was God; let that sink in for a moment. The Word spoke and galaxies were formed, stars flung into their predestined positions, Heavens suddenly materialized, and planets started whirling in their determined order. Those words that He spoke were of magnificent, unrestrained and unlimited power. Lands, animals, plants, mountains. Bodies of water, man and woman were formed with His DNA when He spoke the Word. Incredible! Even more incredible— our words have power, too. By speaking the world into existence, He was modeling for His sons and daughters the creative power of their words.

What kind of power do our words have?

Have you ever thrown a pebble into a body of water and watched as a circle, within a circle, within a circle forms obediently around where the pebble entered the water? How could such a small, seemingly insignificant stone cause such a marked change in the water around it? Our words have that same effect, going into the atmosphere around us and forming scaffoldings of peace or panic, calm or chaos, life or death.

We know God created words to have power. Proverbs 18:21 (NASB) says life and death is in the power of the tongue. Wow, life and death! Science has discovered spoken words each have a frequency or vibration by which they can be measured. Different words have different frequencies. Studies have found that words differ in frequencies *according to their meaning*. For example, think back to a time you were yelled at. Remember that icky feeling of being in trouble, or not measuring up? I recently was in a store and witnessed a mother berating her child. People's attention was drawn to the red face and raised voice of the mother as she shamed the child in front of other staring shoppers. The mood around the mother and her child was changed. I could almost see the thought bubbles forming around the child: "I'm not good enough . . . I can never get anything right . . . I am so bad." If you were to examine the words used in that "conversation," you may find that many of those words had a low frequency of about 200 mhz. However, if you were to utter the name Jesus reverently, the frequency would measure in at about 200,000 mhz.

Japanese scientist Masaru Emoto performed many fascinating experiments to prove the power of spoken words. In two labelled mason jars left in an elementary school classroom, he put white cooked rice. One label said "Thank You" and the other "You Fool." Much to the delight of the students, he instructed them to speak twice a day to each jar of rice what it was labeled with. Within 30 days the "foolish" rice was a black slimy mound while the "thanked" rice was still white and fluffy. Dr Emoto had just proven the power that words have. Dr. Emoto also found that words spoken over water changed the molecule formation of the water. Those are powerful words!

If words of destruction and hate can change the molecular structure of water or cause rice to shrivel and blacken, could our words change the atmosphere around us? Jesus calmed the storm with His words, and said that we will do the same or greater things

(John 14:12 TPT). The words we speak have significance; probably more than we realize. Lies that we agree with and voice frame the atmosphere around us and energizes demonic agreement. Conversely, truths that we voice, words of hope, aspiration, and promise shapes the atmosphere around us and invites the miraculous into our space. The phrase "you are what you eat" is true, but I also think "you are what you say" emanates truth. If you are speaking words of life over yourself and those around you, that is what is being drawn to you. The Lord created us in His image and He spoke the worlds into existence, calmed the weather with His Words, and commanded the lame to "rise up and walk." Are we not to do the same?

The effect of our words

Our words can have different meanings depending on where and when we say them. Where we live in Colorado, wildfires are an unfortunate reality. Someone yelling "fire" sends us into evacuation mode. We are also a state where guns are allowed. Because of tragic church and school shootings here, someone yelling "fire" into a crowd could cause people to take cover, or to pull out their own concealed carry and shoot. We must choose our words carefully as they can have lasting consequences.

What happens when we talk about someone else, or speak lies over ourselves? We fill the atmosphere around us with despair, hopelessness, and defeat. That is not the way the Lord intended His daughters to live life. He created us to speak words of life which creates a platform for His Presence, power and peace to manifest into the atmosphere around us. We are the fragrance of Christ to those perishing (2 Corinthians 2:15 NASB). Could our words be the fragrance we carry with us wherever we go? Our words emit the beautiful scent of the miraculous enabling us and those around us to bloom into all He intended for us to be. That is who I want to be! A daughter of the Most High, who creates beautiful, safe spaces of possibility and strength with her words. Oh, if we encouraged everyone we came in contact with, and spoke over them what Papa God sees when He looks in their eyes—how different would our world be, how different would our daily encounters with others be!

Entrainment and agreement

I recently read a story about two twin girls who were born

premature. One girl had a strong heart and, although she was in an incubator, was thriving. The other twin was very weak and did not have a strong heart. Doctors felt she would not last the night. Going against hospital rules, the strong twin was placed in the same incubator as the weak twin. When nurses checked on them later, the strong twin had placed her arm around the other twin. It was a rescue hug. Slowly, the weak twin's heart started to beat in agreement with her sister, and her heartbeat became strong. The twin girls were eventually able to leave the hospital, both happy and healthy. This is a beautiful example of a scientific principle called entrainment.

A 16th century Dutch scientist named Christian Huygens discovered that if he left identical cuckoo clocks with their pendulums swinging in different directions, the pendulums would eventually adjust themselves to swing in sync with one another. The principle is that two or more objects of the same frequency will lock into phase with one another, a phenomena called entrainment. I once enjoyed watching an episode of MythBusters which demonstrated this principle using metronomes that ticked at different times—after a while, they would tick in sync. All of them would, given a few minutes, become synchronous with one another and swing their pendulums together.

Could Matthew 18:19 (NASB) be calling us into entrainment with what God is saying: "Again I say to you, that if two of you agree on earth about anything that they may ask, it shall be done for them by My Father who is in Heaven"? Our agreement with His words and promises over us brings life. However, our agreement with negative gossip, word curses, and wrong thought patterns brings destruction.

I feel this sometimes happens when you talk with friends. Have you ever found yourself agreeing with a group of friends because you feel it is the thing to do? Speculative words voiced about someone else can gain momentum and quickly turn to gossip as someone is talked about, accused rightly or wrongly, and judged. Agreement fuels the gossip and reputations can quickly get ruined and friendships splintered. It's like we all become those out of sync metronomes that suddenly syncopate with one another and gossip and slander someone who is not there to defend themselves. Gossip slanders someone else. If you can't imagine someone else saying those words to you, to your face; then don't say it about someone else.

Slander devalues someone else and their reputation. However, your hurtful words about someone else wounds your soul, and gives the enemy a legal right to torment you. I call these traps word curses, which are negative words spoken over yourself or others such as, "You are so stupid. You are worthless. You can't get anything right." Agreement with these curses causes alignments and open gateways with the enemy. People often say them out of their own soul wounds, saying them to a child they are frustrated with, or repeating what they heard their parents say over them. We can even say word curses over ourselves, making inner vows: "I'm so stupid. Nobody wants me. I will never let anyone near me again so they can hurt me like so-and-so did." When we come into agreement with these words of death we give the enemy the legal right to torment us further. We build the framework around us by resonating with those word lies and we build a house for the enemy to live right next door! This is the principle of entrainment, but with the enemy. We have to break agreement with those destructive words, which is like demolishing the house we built for the enemy to hang out in.

Entraining to God's Words

There is power in the way we use our words. We slay others with gossip. When we talk negatively about someone, we may persuade others to come into agreement with the way we are thinking about someone and that agreement fuels the atmosphere around them negatively, allowing the demonic to attach to those negative agreements. Proverbs 18:21 (NIV) confirms this: "The tongue has the power of life and death, and those who love it will eat its fruit." In the same way, words have creative power to change the atmosphere for good. Words of praise and thanksgiving can usher in the glory of the Lord to create an atmosphere for hearing His voice and for the miraculous to flow.

Our agreement with His words and promises for us energizes us and brings us life: "For where two or three have gathered together in My name, I am there in their midst" (Matthew 18:20 NASB). When you come into agreement with what God says about you, then those words have creative power to change the atmosphere around you. No longer can the demonic stay around when you are speaking the truth of what Heaven knows about you.

> *Whose words are you entraining to?*

When we come into entrainment with His Truth, our heart beats in unity and oneness with the King of Heaven. What He speaks, you repeat into the earth's atmosphere and circumstances must bend to come into alignment with what Father is declaring over your life! Like the circles-in-circles a pebble makes in a pond, every word counts.

Zephaniah 3:17 says, The Lord your God is in your midst, a warrior who gives victory; He will rejoice over you with gladness and joy, He will renew you in His love; He will exult over you with loud singing (NIV, ESV, ISV). What? Not only does God speak to us, He sings over us. Could He be singing the reality of who you are in Heaven into your DNA? You don't just have a song to sing; you *are* a song!

Geneticists have found it easier to read long strands of DNA code by assigning musical notes to the combinations of amino acids. That means that your DNA becomes a song. You are the only one who has that unique sound. When Cain killed his brother Abel, the Lord said "The voice of your brother's blood is crying to me from the ground" (Genesis 4:10 NASB). If the Word talks about the sound of Abel's blood-song, we all have a special sound that emanates from us. When we speak words of truth, hope and life, we come into agreement with that song. When we speak destructive words, we break entrainment with God's Truth over us and our words become destructive weapons. Our words can become like sonic missiles that hit the target and do great damage to others.

Sonic warfare uses sound to cause disruption, discomfort, dread, and can even generate fear. The US Army used it successfully against Panama leader Manuel Noriega, and now the Air Force is researching high powered micro waves that disrupt and damage targets in seconds. Sound waves are currently used to break up and pulverize kidney stones. A Biblical example of sonic warfare would be the Battle of Jericho. The Lord instructed Joshua to march around Jericho once a day for six days and on the seventh day, to march around the city seven times then blast the atmosphere with a shout from all of Joshua's soldiers and blow ram's horns. The sound caused the walls to crumble down and Joshua captured the city of Jericho. Sound is a weapon. Whose side will you allow to use your sounds?

God's words for us

What does God's voice when He speaks sound like? We may feel His voice may sound like a movie version of a booming male voice, perhaps even with a British accent thrown in for good measure. Elijah found in 1 Kings 19:12 (KJV) God's voice was "still and small," in contrast to the wind, earthquake, and fire he was trying to hear Him in. Samuel thought God's voice calling him was actually his teacher Eli's voice in 1 Samuel 3. In Jeremiah 23:29 (NIV) God says, "Is not my word like fire . . . and like a hammer that breaks the rock in pieces?" Psalm 29:3-9 (NASB) talks about how the voice of God thunders, is powerful and full of majesty, breaks the cedars, splits and flashes forth like lightening, makes the wilderness tremble, causes deer to give birth immediately, twists the oaks, strips the forest bare, and causes everyone in the temple to cry out "Glory!" Psalm 46:6 (NASB) says His voice causes the earth to melt. Yikes. I think we can agree that whenever God speaks, every molecule in the universe begins to respond to His voice. The whole universe was brought into being by His prophetic declaration. God spoke everything into existence!

The planets even emit a sound, as He commanded them to. NASA has released a recording called "Symphonies of the Planets," which is composed of recordings made by Voyager 1 and 2, as they cruised by different planets in the solar system. Each planet gives off a signature sound in the form of electromagnetic waves which is convertible to an audible and recognizable song. The planets are just being obedient to what the Lord commanded in Psalm 148:3 (NIV): "Praise Him, sun and moon, praise Him all you shining stars." That is exactly what the planets are doing! These are the sounds that God's created universe sing.

I have wondered what Jesus' voice sounded like when He told Lazarus to come out of the grave, even though he had been in there for 3 days. Did He whisper, did He raise His voice, every word articulated—"Lazarus, come forth!" Well, however it sounded, Lazarus gathered himself up and out he obediently walked, no doubt with grave clothes and rotting flesh. Jesus spoke to a fig tree and told it that it would never bear fruit again, and it immediately withered. What must that have sounded like? I wonder what the tenor of His voice was after He was awoken from a deep sleep by the frantic disciples and said "Peace, be still" to the storm? The storm certainly aligned with his words, as it immediately stilled. When Jesus commanded the sick and crippled to be healed, their bodies came into alignment and immediately responded to His command. Jesus tells us in John 14:12 (TPT) that if we believe in Him, we will do the same mighty miracles he did, and even greater! John 15:7 (NIV) says, "if you remain in me and my words remain in you, ask whatever you wish, and it will be given you." God's words are powerful, but our words have power and we can learn to wield those word missiles for good and not for evil.

Sometimes it may be difficult to come into agreement with what God is saying. Because we have learned how to speak negatively about ourselves, our circumstances, and others, it takes a conscious effort on our part to break out of that habit and learn to speak God's Truths into the atmosphere around us. We must never discount the power of our agreement with His words. There is power in our "yes" to Him. We see that so vividly with Mary, the mother of Jesus. Mary came into entrainment with the fantastical visit by the angel Gabriel who told this virgin teenager that she would be impregnated with the Son of God. I am continually stunned by Mary's answer. The Passion Translation records her response: "This is amazing! I will be a mother for the Lord! As his servant, I accept whatever he has for me. May everything you have told me come to pass" (Luke 1:38). That is one powerful yes!

What if Mary would have said no; if she was not on board with what God proposed? Have you felt out of your comfort zone when God asks you to agree with something He says about you? Maybe you cannot wrap your head around what He says about you: *You are wanted, beautiful, valued, gifted, needed, and loved* (just to list a few things). Maybe He has asked you to do something you feel unqualified to do. When we embrace saying yes to what He says to us and about us, we come into entrainment with His heart for us.

Could we say that if we come into agreement with what God is saying, then Heaven and earth responds to the sounds we speak? What do you want to be known for: words of life, agreement with Heaven, words that have to power to destroy chains of the enemy in other's lives? I think so! I want to carry that creativity in my words and release words of life over others, myself, and the atmosphere around me. When we come into agreement with what God is saying over us and the world around us, we are speaking with Heaven's frequency. Then, we make the same resonance through our words that God makes. Your words have the power to start and stop wars in your life, in your head, among your friends, your sphere of influence, and the very atmosphere around you. Speak what God is saying. Speak it over your life and over those around you, into your circumstances, your heartaches, your triumphs. When we agree, resonate, and speak God's words, we activate the miraculous around us and nothing is impossible!

Prayer:

Father, I acknowledge that I have not always spoken words of life over myself and others. Forgive me for knowingly and unknowingly gossiping or speaking unkindly about someone. Forgive me for coming into agreement and speaking words of death over myself. I repent and ask for Your forgiveness. I renounce all agreement with any word curses spoken over me by someone else or myself. I break its power in Jesus name. Help me to choose my words carefully so they bring life and speak Your truth. I want to frame the atmosphere around me with your Truth and possibility. In Jesus Name, Amen.

Activation:

Settle yourself in a quiet time with the Lord. Thank Him for the power of His Words. Ask the Lord what He says about you. Write down what you are hearing. Ask Him for scriptures that have been special promises to you as you have walked through difficult circumstances in your life. Write those down, too. Declare over yourself what the Lord is saying about you and come into agreement with those truths.

Huddle Questions:

1. Explain a time when you experienced the power of words that were life giving.

2. Discuss some strategies you may use to help you speak words that are in agreement with Heaven.

3. Take this next week to consciously listen to the way you talk when you are interacting with others. Are your words positive and life-

giving? Are they recalling truth or agreeing with lies or half-truths? At the end of the week evaluate how you want the following week to look via your conversations. Ask Holy Spirit for help and guidance how to adjust your words so they are life giving.

Girls With Gumption: Evangeline Booth

Christmas brings many traditions, and the red kettle of the Salvation Army bell ringers outside stores is one such tradition. Evangeline Booth, daughter of William and Catherine Booth who founded the Salvation Army, was born on Christmas day 1865 in London England. The Salvation Army was formed to help meet the needs of the poor in London but spread worldwide demonstrating the love and compassion of the Lord. From a young age, Evangeline was taught by her family that men and women could be used equally by God. Eva was a fervent evangelist and when still a child started a Doll Hospital and invited the neighborhood children to bring their broken dolls. While a neighbor mended the dolls, Evangeline shared God's love with the customers. By 17 she was preaching, having a flair for music and the dramatic which she showcased with her dramatized Bible Stories and songs. For a period, she lived and served in the slums of England, dressed in tattered clothes to minister to the poor. She was nicknamed "The White Angel of the Slums." She developed the reputation as a force for the Lord and whenever there were challenging and tricky circumstances the Salvation Army faced, her father and founder William Booth would say "Send Eva!"

At 22, she was appointed Field Commander of Great Britain. Later she became the Territorial Leader of Canada, and in 1904 she was elected as Commander of United States Salvation Army. Under her leadership, she developed disaster relief programs. After the great San Francisco Earthquake of 1906, she raised significant funds to help the disaster victims. She helped establish soup kitchens, emergency shelters, hospitals for unwed mothers, unemployment aid, homes for the aged, and prison ministry. During World War I, she sent Salvationists to the front lines to minister. In 1919 she was awarded the Distinguished Service Metal by President Woodrow Wilson. In 1934 she was elected as the first woman General of the Salvation Army. By then the Salvation Army's scope reached into 80 countries. She served as Commander in Chief for 5 years before retiring. In 1950 she preached her last sermon entitled "The Love of God," and died later that year. Evangeline once described the work of the Salvation Army as "an army of men and women who cry in all the languages of the earth, 'Behold the Lamb of God who taketh away the sins of the world.'" Her Army continues on, leaving a legacy of devotion, evangelism and meeting needs of others in His Name. This Warrior Princess saw others through the eyes of compassion, motivated and activated by the love of God.

6

Taking Every Thought Captive

"As we think, we change the physical nature of our brain. As we consciously direct our thinking, we can wire out toxic patterns of thinking and replace them with healthy thoughts."

– Dr. Caroline Leaf

I was driving the other day and was distracted by the incredible mountain views we have in our city. The mountains are literally right there. I noted there was snow on Pikes Peak, which was weirdly juxtaposed with the blooming flower bed in the median as I stopped at a red light. Brilliantly bright flowers were set against the backdrop of a majestic snowcapped mountain. A plastic grocery bag blown up and down by the wind nonchalantly drifted by. I watched it traverse across the lanes of traffic, wrap around a light post, and then fly free like it was in a hurry to get somewhere. Sometimes my thoughts can be like that plastic bag. They take me all over the place. I can think on an errand I have to run and end up remembering something that happened to me in 6th grade. It is crazy. Are you like that too? Sometimes I need my errant and scattered thoughts, that are like crazy, excited honey bees, to be brought back to the hive and just chill.

Our thoughts can get us into trouble. I once heard it said that as women, we tend to put every thought we have into the washing machine of our mind and it gets all jumbled up together. Men tend to keep everything in neat compartments, like many doors that line a hallway, each room being a different aspect of their thoughts. Interesting. I don't know if this is true or not, and that certainly doesn't pertain to everyone, but it could help explain why when I argue with my husband about the color we are going to paint our walls, I bring up an incident that happened when we were dating. In any case, our thoughts can quickly turn destructive and damaging. There is a struggle that goes on in our mind.

Our mind can sometimes be a dark and twisty place, fueled by anxious thoughts about the future—*Will I ever meet someone to spend the rest of my life with? Will I have enough money to cover rent this month? How will I be reconciled with my friend I am in a fight with?* Or, you may also be thinking, *How can I stop thinking pornographic thoughts? I am not enough. How could anyone ever love the real me?* . . . You get the picture. Our thoughts can house our greatest hopes and dreams, and they can also quickly catapult us into dark places of replaying images of trauma or caustic conversations causing a downward spiraling of worry and anxiety. Our mind is a battlefield.

The war of the mind

The number one way the enemy comes to mess with us is in our mind, in our thoughts. His main objective is to get us to forget who we really are. We then come into alignment with his lies and he has succeeded in the battle for our mind. He is the original identity thief. He is fearful if we really understand, comprehend and live out our true identity as a Warrior Princess, we will be, in the words of 17th century author Madame Jeanne Guyon, "a more formidable opponent than any army ready for war." The enemy is threatened by our thought life. Wow. That is why there seems to be such a battle in our mind. Truth verses lies. Which one are you allowing to win?

In the battle for your mind, who is gaining the most ground?

Author and speaker Joyce Meyer once said, "There is a war going on, and your mind is the battlefield. But the good news is that God is fighting on your side." The struggle is real. It is often challenging keeping our stuff together and not allowing our thoughts to run willy-nilly. I feel sometimes our thoughts can be like a big gust of wind on a fall day, which carry the just-raked, colored leaves up and away in a haphazard wind vortex. Sometimes it's hard to settle ourselves down and call all those frantic thoughts back into the leaf pile. It takes practice. Left unattended, our thoughts can create multitudes of problems and cause us to align ourselves with lies which leads us to become spiritually, emotionally, and physically out of calibration. Remember the concept of entrainment from last chapter? Yeah, your thought life is a huge battleground for that.

We can carry whole conversations with ourselves in our mind. We can give ourselves a pep talk, tell ourselves everything is going to be ok, or we can work ourselves up into a frenzy of worry, anxiousness, and despair. I want to be the pep talk girl in my mind. I want to be the cheerleader, telling myself that I am enough and everything is going to be ok, despite what the circumstances around me might say. However, it is all too easy to do the opposite and allow feelings of anxiety, rage, jealousy—you can pick your poison—to consume us. How easy it is to fall down a rabbit hole of worry and anxiety and get ourselves worked up into a frenzy. Have you been there? The Lord knows that we tend towards that. David expressed in Psalm 94:19 (NASB), "When my anxious thoughts multiply within me, Your consolations delight my soul." It seems that our mind has a mind of its own. So how does a thought form, grow, and multiply?

Anatomy of a thought

My daughter is taking Anatomy and Physiology at her college. The amount of information she has to learn is incredible. She can tell us about any body part and the bones and muscles that make up that particular part of the body. The human anatomy is amazing. That makes me think about the anatomy of a thought. How does it start, and how is it energized to have such potent power? A thought germinates in our mind and once we allow it to grow, it gives way to a corresponding emotion. For example, we might see it snowing outside, and think that driving could be hazardous, and you could get in an accident thus allowing fear to become attached to that thought. This is one I am familiar with! So what is the actual science behind how our brain forms a thought and emotion?

I grew up in Canada where we enjoyed snow for what seems like half the year. Well-worn pathways in the snow told the story of where our friends lived, where the dog liked to do their business, or the pathway to the mailbox. Those well-travelled pathways would be stamped into the snow and become easy to walk on. So it is with a thought. An electrical signal travels between neurons and makes a pathway for a thought. A neuron is basically a nerve cell, of which we have about a hundred billion in our brain. Our thoughts are constantly changing the structure of our brain. This is called neuron plasticity (*neuro* for brain, *plasticity* for changing). Researchers have found our thoughts look like trees, complete with branches. Dr. Caroline Leaf talks about this in her wonderful book, *Who Switched Off My Brain?*. The branches of those "trees" are constantly growing all the time, depending on what type of thought is feeding them. A toxic thought or memory produces tree branches that look like a ghoulish tree from a Halloween movie, while a healthy thought or memory produces a healthy-looking tree in our brain. We are thinking beings and we can choose to build a healthy thought or a toxic thought. These thoughts then can cause us to act depending on the nature of the thought and can release chemical reactions in our bodies. Essentially, the emotions that transpire from a thought release chemicals into our body. The warm fuzzy feeling of happiness which is generated by thinking of a favorite memory is contrasted by the sick feeling in the pit of your stomach caused by a discouraging or heart-breaking thought. There is no doubt that your thought life greatly affects your emotions, and your physical health.

There is a gland in our brain called the hypothalamus gland which connects our mind and nervous system to the rest of the body and allows the body to listen in on what is going on in the mind. This means that the toxic thoughts we entertain can negatively affect our nervous system, which affects our health. It is estimated 87% of illness is a direct result of our thoughts.[5] Our thoughts have power. Research has revealed that our thoughts can cause even our DNA to change shape.[6]

Thoughts' effect on the body

I have a problem with paper. The receipt kind. I have receipts for every purchase I've made probably for the last 10 years. I've collected and kept birthday cards for my kids, notes people have written me, utility bills I've paid from 6 years ago—you get the picture. Could our body hold on to our thoughts and keep a record of it?

Actually, yes! Scientists have found that your DNA holds a

record of everything that you have been through in your life. And that's a lot: "One gram of DNA can store 700 terabytes of data. To store the same kind of data on hard drives—the densest storage medium in use today—you'd need 233 three-terabyte drives, weighing a total of 151 kilos (about 333 pounds).[7]

That would mean that our bodies keep a record of our thoughts. Knowing this makes me want to try to only record healthy, positive thoughts. 3 John 1:2 (KJV) says "Beloved, I wish above all things that you may prosper and be in health, even as your soul prospers." I love this verse and I embrace the idea I can have a healthy and prosperous soul which is fed and nourished by thinking about Truth and not coming into agreement with lies. The dictionary meaning of *prosper* is to flourish, grow strong, healthy, thrive, bloom, blossom, and progress. Yes, please. I don't want to just survive, like the plastic bag that makes it across the freeway without getting stuck under someone's tire; I want the fullness of 3 John 1:2 that allows my soul to flourish, bloom, and prosper.

A healthy thought life

How do we work towards a soul like 3 John 1:2 describes? By weighing out the value of our thoughts and deciding if we want to go down that bunny trail. Is it healthy for us to think about those things? We want a healthy soul which makes healthy decisions, that has healthy emotions, doesn't fantasize about things that are false.

Philippians 4:8 (TPT) tells us "so keep your thoughts continually fixed on all that is authentic and real, honorable and admirable, beautiful and respectful, pure and holy, merciful and kind. And fasten your thoughts on every glorious work of God, praising Him always." Well, sometimes that is easier said than done. Can I get an Amen!? Paul laments about this in Romans 7:20 (NASB) when he says, "But if I am doing the very thing I do not want, I am no longer the one doing it, but sin which dwells in me." When our soul becomes wounded, our thoughts get out of control and we spiral down into a vortex of wrong thinking and agreement with lies. We can replay scenarios of wounding on the television screen of our minds, causing us to relive those dark moments and come into agreement with those reanimated hopeless feelings and lies.

The television screen in our minds is a very powerful place. It can be the place of encountering the Lord during worship, or can also be the place of fantasy. There could be a boy you like and so you fantasize how he would pursue you, declare his love for you, make grand gestures of love in front of your friends, including your old boyfriends, and, thrown in for good measure, girls who have been mean to you! Suddenly we have superimposed on this person a fantasy character who may possess none of the qualities we are fantasizing about them. They may not be kind, or good, or even have any interest in you. Your old boyfriends may not be jealous of him (if he even existed in real life), and all the mean girls may still just roll their eyes and turn their backs to you. It is just a fantasy, in your mind.

Maybe you have been rejected by someone and you imagine all the bad things that would happen to them. Or you may have been betrayed by someone and you fantasize about how you can exact revenge. All of these thoughts reroute your neural freeways, like those pathways in the snow. It may cause you to dwell on toxic and caustic thoughts that cause you to feel sick, cause your emotions to get out of whack, and may even cause you to act out uncharacteristically.

Proverbs 4:23 (NLT) says guard your heart above all else, for it determines the course of your life. The New American Standard Bible puts it this way: "Watch over your heart with all diligence, for from it flow the springs of life." The Hebrew word for *heart* in that verse also translates to mind. If we are watching over our mind, then that would mean we would be policing our thoughts and our fantasy life. Paul tells us in 2 Corinthians 10:5 (TPT) that, "we can demolish every deceptive fantasy that opposes God and break through every arrogant attitude that is raised up in defiance of the true knowledge of God. We capture, like prisoners of war, every thought and insist it bow in obedience to the Anointed One."

> "My child, pay attention to what I say. Listen carefully to my words. Don't lose sight of them. Let them penetrate deep into your heart, for they bring life to those who find them, and healing to their whole body. Guard your heart above all else, for it determines the course of your life."
> (Proverbs 4:20-23 NLT)

How exactly are we taking every thought captive when we allow our mind to dwell on things that are corrosive? The Lord is not adding this to a list of don'ts, but it is protection like putting ointment on a bad burn. Keeping our thoughts healthy causes our soul to prosper. If we continue to allow accusatory and destructive thinking, it causes chaos in our mind. If you allow these cycles to play on a loop, you feel like pandemonium is taking over and you cannot calm your mind down and dwell in peace. Before it gets to that level, get control of what you are allowing your mind to dwell on. In other words, nip it in the bud.

What if your thoughts have spiraled so out of control, you cannot reign them back in?

Firstly, ask the Lord where that thought was first allowed to enter. What was the open door; was it because of sin, trauma, or an event that happened? A trauma that takes place in our life can cause us to align with lies, and that becomes part of our identity until that agreement is broken.

For example, if your boyfriend breaks up with you and you are blindsided, you may feel that you were rejected and agree with the lie "I am not enough," or, "I am unlovable." That lie becomes part of your identity and can bleed over into other scenarios. You may see an Instagram post of friends getting together and you were not invited. That could trigger the thought that you were left out, rejected, not wanted. You get the picture. The reality of it is that the friend may have bumped into one another spontaneously and taken a picture. You were not purposely left out. However, that lie has been activated because your thoughts are stewing over your breakup so you now think everyone is purposely rejecting you, everywhere you turn. That is simply not true, but it feels true to you. That lie has now been invited to take up residence in your thoughts and has festered into a soul wound. Perhaps they did leave you out, however. Allowing a second lie to enter the picture, you believe, "I am not wanted." This deepens your wound even further with more lies.

Now what? Sit with Jesus and ask Him where that deepest lie was allowed to enter. Repent and ask forgiveness for allowing that lie to take up residence in your thoughts. You may be asking, why do you have to ask forgiveness, if it was someone else that did the damage to you? That may be true but you are holding yourself in bondage by agreeing with the lie and holding on to unforgiveness toward that other person. I've heard it said that holding onto unforgiveness is like drinking poison and expecting the other person to die! No one wins in this scenario, and God is heartbroken over the lies you have believed. Repent, forgive, and walk towards your freedom: God says, "You are enough for Me," He loves you, and He wants you.

Next, plead the Blood of Jesus over that soul wound. His Blood always speaks a better Word. (Hebrews 12:24 NIV) His Blood cleans and disinfects the wound and causes healing to begin. One tiny drop of our blood contains our history and even future of our health. If our blood tells us all that, imagine the power of a single drop of Jesus' blood! It heals, delivers and recalibrates us. His Blood restores and rejuvenates.

Then, apply the *dunamis* power of the Lord to the wound. The *dunamis* power is the same word used in Luke 9:1 when Jesus called His disciples together and gave them power (*dunamis*) and authority over demons and to heal diseases. It is also used in Luke 8:9 when the woman with the issue of blood touches Jesus' robe and He says that He felt power (*dunamis*) go out of Him. It means the power to perform miracles, moral power, and excellence of soul. It is like putting special healing cream on that wound which causes it to heal quickly. Imagine the warmth of the Son healing the wound completely so it is as if it never existed! Imagine our mind being cleansed of all wrong agreements and lies we have covenanted with. How would that look? Would we be able to finally see, agree and live in our true identity as His Daughter? He did not create us to live in bondage to lies of the enemy and trapped in unforgiveness. Yet so often that is just what we are content to do.

That is not how the Lord created our mind to be used, to be in a constant state of worry and anxiety and negative thinking. Romans 12:2 holds a key: "Do not conform any longer to the pattern of this world, but be transformed by the renewing of your mind" (AMP, NIV). The word transformed in Greek is *metamorphoo*, which you probably notice looks like our word metamorphosis. That same word was chosen in Matthew 17:2 and Mark 9:2 to describe the transfiguration of Jesus. Jesus took Peter, James and John up a high mountain. Here's how The Passion Translation tells the story of Mark 9:2-3: "And Jesus' appearance was dramatically altered, for he was transfigured before their very eyes! His clothing sparkled and became glistening white—whiter than any bleach in the world could make them." That must have been quite a sight! What could the Word be alluding to about our thoughts being transformed? Romans 12:2 continues saying our thinking will be transformed by the renewing of our mind. The Greek word for renewing translates to renovation, rejuvenation, the process and work of restoring something back to a new condition. Perhaps that is what the Lord has in store for us as we submit our thoughts to His renewal process;

we get a makeover!

Paul so eloquently tells us in Ephesians 4:23-24 (TPT), "Now it's time to be made new by every revelation that's been given to you. And to be transformed as you embrace the glorious Christ-within as your new life and live in union with him! For God has re-created you all over again in his perfect righteousness, and you now belong to him in the realm of true holiness." I love that. We get a do over. There is no place your thoughts have taken you that cannot be renewed. You are not beyond rescuing; your mind is not such a dark place that He cannot shine His Truth and Peace. He is in the business of literally renewing us in the spirit of our mind. Yes, please!

Victory on the battlefield

It is so interesting to consider we could get a mind makeover; a tune up and transformation of our mind and thinking. Our "yes" to Him in this aspect has wonderful ramifications. For then we remove the enemy's definition of who he has labeled us to be: not enough, rejected, unlovable, you fill in the blank. The battle may be in our mind, but His Presence brings peace and victory to every place of hand to hand combat defeat with the enemy we have experienced. As we submit our mind and thoughts to God and take every thought captive, He increases in us and energizes our mind with the renewing of His Word. We war with the enemy by guarding our connection with Him. If the enemy returns to our renovated mind, there is no place for him any longer and he has to leave. We have thrown his stuff out on the front lawn and changed the locks. No more do we entertain the enemy's lies allowing us to come into bondage but we have broken free and are enjoying our made-over mind space.

Some days will be better than others. Some circumstances may derail us and we find ourselves going back into the familiar destructive thought patterns. Take a breath. Turn into Jesus. Reconnect with His Presence. Drink in His Peace, meditate on His Word and allow Him to resynchronize your thinking as He whispers into your spirit who you are in Him. Live a lifestyle of living in His Presence, causing the insistent chatter of lies from the enemy to grow fainter and fainter until you can't hear them any longer. The false identity attached to the lies is transformed like a butterfly breaking out of their cocoon into the Truth of who you really are. Our thoughts now become a gateway into His Presence. Our mind which once held toxic thought patterns and destructive fantasy is cleaned out, rearranged and cleansed to hold His Presence. Our once dark and twisty mind now is able to house the Prince of Peace. Our imagination now becomes a place of encounter with the King of Glory. It becomes a place where we are never alone, where our anxious thoughts can be hushed by His reassuring, life-giving voice. That is how I want to live. That is how I want to think. I will not allow my thoughts to be like a plastic bag driven by the haphazard winds of the enemy and vortex of my own making, and if I do, I will turn to Him and get back on track. I choose to live in His Presence and entertain peace, hope, and joy in the renovated living room of my mind. I will serve them fragrant tea, watch old home movies of happy memories, and brainstorm with them all the plans He has for me. 1 Corinthians 2:16 (NLT) promises me "For we have the mind of Christ." I believe I do, and so should you.

Prayer:

Lord I invite you into my imagination gateway. Stand next to me and be the doorkeeper to all my thoughts. I ask that Your Blood would cleanse every place where I have allowed a pathway of destructive thoughts to form. Erase that corrosive pathway and wash it clean like fresh fallen snow. Help me create new healthy pathways. I invite Your glory fire to burn away all painful memories I play over in my mind which cause me to become stuck in repetitive cycles of shame, rejection, hopelessness, and anything else which is not of You. I want my mind to be the place I meet with You. Thank You that You say I have the mind of Christ. I desire my thoughts to be submitted to You. Amen.

Activation:

I want you to imagine a large door in front of you. It could be the door to your own house. Do you see the door handle? Reach for it and open it. Imagine walking across the threshold of the door and step inside. In Revelation 3:20, Jesus tells us He knocks at the door and all we need to do is turn the handle and open the door so we can hang out with Him. Imagine opening the door and seeing Jesus standing in the doorway. Maybe you can't see Him but You can sense His Presence. What are you feeling, what are you seeing, hearing, smelling, and even tasting? Allow yourself to imagine experiencing Him via all those senses. Can you feel His love, His approval,

His nearness? Practice this exercise over and over, for you could experience Him differently every time. What is He saying to you? Bring your anxieties and cares to Him and allow Him to tell you what He is saying about your circumstances. There is no right or wrong way to do this. Enjoy visiting with Him.

Huddle Questions:

1. What are some ways destructive thought patterns can affect our actions?

2. What role does the media (social media, movies, YouTube, etc.) play in contributing to unhealthy thought processes?

3. Moving forward, what plan can you put in place to capture your toxic thoughts?

Girls with Gumption:
Jeanne Guyon

Madame Jeanne Guyon is forever remembered for one thing, her secret life with God. Born in the 1600s to a wealthy French Roman Catholic family, she was sent away as a child by her mother and lived at various Benedictine convents until her teens. It was there she fell in love with knowing and understanding God's love for herself and others.

Hungry for more of Him, she developed a love of prayer and communing with God. A beautiful girl, she was tricked into an arranged marriage at 15 years old. Driven to desperation by an abusive marriage, a cruel mother in law, and critical mother, Jeanne cried out to the Lord from the depths of her being. At nineteen, after the birth of two children, she met a monk whose face glowed from the Presence of God. She started spending time at the monastery, tutored by the monk. Her depth of intimacy with the Lord grew as she eagerly received Heavenly revelation of dwelling in the secret place. Time removed its constraints and Jeanne would be lost in prayer for hours. Sadly, her husband became jealous and her tutor, betrayed her, and said she was delusional. Her family felt she spent too much time praying and forbid it. Through the storm of her family's harsh persecution, and an almost fatal case of smallpox which disfigured her beautiful face, Jeanne would constantly return to the depths of peace and rest in the Lord through prayer.

Jeanne wrote of her experiences and encounters with the Lord and these works remain classics. Some of these writings led to her imprisonment. Charged as a heretic, she was forced to write her theological beliefs as penance, gifting us with some of her most profound insights. Finally released and allowed to live out the rest of her days communing with her Beloved Heavenly Bridegroom, Madame Jeanne Guyon's relationship with the Lord still brings encouragement to many today. This Warrior Princess' writings remain a way for countless followers to find their way to the secret place of His Presence. Her life of utter devotion and love for God is a map which points us to finding the treasure of an intimate relationship with our Redeemer.

7

What are You Packing?

"When I stand before God at the end of my life, I would hope that I would not have a single bit of talent left and could say, 'I used everything You gave me.'"

– Erma Bombeck

I don't know if you are like I am, but I find it stressful and difficult to pack for a trip. I often leave it until the last minute. There are so many unknowns to factor in! What will the weather be like, what will I be doing, what will everyone else be wearing? Inquiring minds want to know. Well, maybe just my inquiring mind. A lot of the time, I feel like I do not pack the right things. I lament why didn't I pack my favorite grey sweater, because it would be perfect right about now in this freezing-cold, air-conditioned restaurant, or why didn't I pack my comfy jeans because evidently I ate too much in the freezing-cold restaurant trying to stay warm and now my current jeans don't fit! You get the picture.

This problem is replicated with what is in my purse. I try to fill my purse with things I think I might need as I travel around town running errands, meeting with friends, attending appointments. An injured back necessitated my scaling down of my luggage sized purse to something much smaller. It required a paring down of my makeup collection I toted around to one lipstick and one gloss. Other important decisions needed to be made until I came up with a small purse that just held the necessities. It took a while to get used to, but now with my teeny purse and its scaled-down contents, I feel equipped for most any challenge.

That's packing for just a day, or a few hours. Imagine packing all you would ever need. That's basically what a hope chest is— packing a chest for a new life. I remember being intrigued with my mother's hope chest. She carefully selected what would be deemed worthy of finding a home in the beautiful wooden box lined with cedar. Every time you lifted the lid, the beautiful, fragrant, cedarwood smell would fill the air. My mom received the hope chest as a teenager, and in it she placed all the precious gifts others had given to her to be used once she was married, or moved away and had a home of her own. In it she had embroidered linens, crystal, china, silverware, tablecloths, kitchen tools, and many other things that would help her to set a beautiful table and make her home comfortable. That is like packing for a really long trip; moving to your own place.

> *Imagine packing for all you would ever need.*

Do you know that the Lord has given us a hope chest? In it, He has placed everything His Bride would need to lead a victorious life in Him! It contains a tremendous arsenal. Imagine with me that together we are going to lift the lid of that hope chest and start to take out the weapons He has placed in there for us, and discover how to use each one. These weapons are not for us to only admire, but to actually put to good use. Unlike crystal and crocheted place mats, we are called to war with these weapons.

Why War?

Why does the Bride need to go to war? Is she not just supposed to sit in the inner chamber and look pretty, safe with her hope chest and doilies? The grime and gore of battle are for the Rescuer, the Knight. Why should the Bride get involved? How could a hope chest possibly help in a war? Well, the Lord wants to change our image. Both the battlefield and the inner chambers are fair game in this war, against this enemy. And, the Bride is a powerful force, be it on the battlefield or from her inner chambers, for it is from a place of intimacy that the Bride wars. That's what His hope chest for us is all about.

You may be a warfare casualty. Sickness, disappointment, broken relationships, inner hurts, and other foes may have left you defeated, dejected, and exhausted. Even well-meaning friends might have chided you for standing on the battlefield in the first place. Sound familiar? We need to learn to war from a place of intimacy and rest, not of ignorance and naivety.

Remember this: This time of warfare is one where the battle has already been won. We choose from the multiple weapons in our holsters and strategically shoot our foe in the places of weakness that have been identified. You see, we have been in a briefing with the Captain of the Hosts. In fact, we are very familiar with this inner counsel chamber. We get the strategy from the Lord, and then use the high-tech weapons from our hope chest to decimate our opponent. Let's imagine you open your hope chest to see a whole host of items—a cup and a plate, a music box, a scroll, a tube of lipstick, some battle clothes, and a telephone, among others. Let's pull these weapons out and see what you're packing.

Unveiling Our Weapons: the Cup

Let's reach into our hope chest and pull out our first weapon. It is the blood of Jesus represented by a communion cup. What a beautiful and powerful weapon this is. Scientists can now take a single drop of blood and tell us what diseases we are genetically predisposed to, what our health is like, what we eat, and if we are stressed. You can determine your history by examining your blood, but we need to remember that our *future* is in the blood of King Jesus.

Leviticus 17:11 (NASB) says, "For the life of the flesh is in the blood; and I have given it to you upon the altar to make atonement for your souls: for it is the blood by reason of the life that makes atonement." There is life in the blood. You can bleed to death and lose your life. God ingeniously created the blood so that life is in our physical blood, and eternal, cleansing, healing life is in the blood of Jesus.

In Hebrew, the word blood means *nephesh*, or life. We are living examples of that life. In the Old Testament, when someone sinned, they needed the *nephesh* of another animal to cover their sin. Jesus' blood covers or atones for us. The word atonement is *kaphar* which means covering. He is our covering.

In Exodus 12, the children of Israel were instructed to smear the blood of a lamb on the doorposts of their houses. This was a type and shadow of the blood of Jesus. If the blood of a lamb protected the Israelites from the power of death, how much more does the precious blood of Jesus protect us?

You may have heard people say "I plead the blood of Jesus." While you won't find this phrase in the Bible, we can see the principle in the Word. The Israelites applied the blood to their doorposts. They could have kept the lamb in the house as they were instructed to, and then killed it. However, if the blood was not applied to their door, then there was no protection.

In Exodus 24:8 (NASB) Moses took the blood, sprinkled it on the people and said "This is the blood of the covenant." The people who have blood on them are sanctified or set apart for God. That means if you touch them, then you touch what is God's. He has put His mark of ownership on us. We belong to Him and whoever messes with His princess, messes with the Prince.

Jesus was the Lamb, slain before the foundation of the world, before lambs were even created. In Revelation 5:6 (NASB), He is a Lamb standing "as if slain." Heaven is constantly reminded of His shed blood and it is a powerful tool against the enemy.

Satan hates the blood. He was an angel initially, so there was no blood in him; and, he cannot be covered with the blood of Jesus. It is the blood of Jesus that defeats him.

> "They overcame him because of the blood of the Lamb, and because of the word of their testimony and they did not love their life even to death."
> (Revelation 12:11 NASB)

We need to apply the blood of Jesus over our problems, our circumstances, our families, our household, our neighborhood, our children's school, and over our place of work. The blood of Jesus is a power weapon in defeating the enemy.

Unveiling our Weapons: the Scroll

The second weapon in our hope chest we pull out is a scroll, and on it is written the names of God. Biblically, names unlock the revelation of character, marked an event in history, or a name was changed for an important reason.

When God used names in the Bible, He used them for a specific reason. For example, the meaning of names used in the book of Ruth divulges a new layer of understanding. Naomi came from Bethlehem-Judah which means "place of bountiful provision and joy." Naomi and her husband Elimelich moved to Moab, which means "place of calamity" and this resulted in the terrible loss of the presence of God for their family. Her husband and sons all died there and Naomi was anxious to get back home to Bethlehem which means "house of bread." She was hungry for God's presence. The name Naomi means pleasant, yet when she had lost her husband and sons she changed her name to Mara which means bitter. A study of names reveals hidden meanings in Scripture.

When women get married, they often take on the name of their spouse. If the last name is famous or well known, then it could characterize the qualities or deeds of that family. For example, the name Billy Graham is well known. His children Franklin and Anne Graham Lotz have inherited their father's pendant for preaching as well as his last name.

I remember when I got married and took my husband's last name of Wright. I was teaching high school at the time and went from being called Miss Reimer by the students in June, to Mrs. Wright in September. I had a new name. This new name appeared on my new credit cards, and because of who I was married to, my credit limit went up!

Philippians 2:9-10 (NASB) says, "Therefore also God has highly exalted Him and bestowed on Him the name which is above every name, that in the name of Jesus every knee should bow, of those who are in heaven and on earth and under the earth and every tongue should confess that Jesus Christ is Lord to the glory of God the Father." Jesus is a powerful name. It is the most powerful name in the world, and it belongs to our King. If it belongs to Him and we are His Bride, then we can use that name and all that His name entails.

There is power, salvation and healing in the name of Jesus. The disciples used the name of Jesus and people were healed. In Acts 3:6, Peter commanded a crippled man, "In the name of Jesus, walk." The man did just that. Acts 4:12 (NASB) says, "And there is salvation in no one else, for there is no other name under Heaven that has been given among men by which we must be saved." John 14:14 (NASB) states "If you ask anything in My name, I will do it."

The name of Jesus declares His character, what He can and will do and all that He has done. His name is a powerful weapon of our warfare. The authority in His name backs us wherever we go.

Imagine that a policeman walked to the middle of a busy street during rush hour. He held up his hand and cars stopped. Why did they stop? They stopped because the policeman had the authority to stop traffic. He had the authority of his precinct, of his city, and of the government behind him. When we use the name of Jesus as a weapon, we have the authority of all of heaven behind that name. We are His beloved and when we use His name it has the power to heal and deliver.

We can use the name of Jesus as a powerful weapon to defeat the enemy. We can also use the meanings of the many names of God as a weapon. The meanings of those names hold a treasure chest of power and anointing that is available to us, the bearer of His name. We, as His Bride are entitled to prophetically declare the fulfillment of the names of God over our lives and over our circumstances.

The Lord uses His name throughout the Word to reveal various aspects of His personality and nature. Every name of God unveils an aspect of His character. There are over 350 names of God in the Bible.[8] By understanding Who He is we are better able to comprehend who we are in Him. God is faithful to His name, and the meanings of His name are binding covenants. He cannot act contrary to His name. He is the Ancient of Days, Beautiful, Bread of Life, Commander of the Army of the Lord, Consuming Fire, Deliverer, Ever-Present, Fortress, Good Shepherd, Healer, our Intercessor, Jehovah Jireh (Our Provider), Jehovah M'Kaddesh (Our Sanctification), Jehovah Nissi (Our Banner), Jehovah Rohi (Our Shepherd), Jehovah Rophe (Our Healer), Jehovah Shammah (Ever Present), Jehovah Shalom (Our Peace), Jehovah Tsidkenu (Our Righteousness), King of Glory, Lion of Judah, Majestic, Name Above All Names, Overcomer, Protector, Quieter of the Storm, Rescuer, Strength, Truth, Unchanging, Vindicator, Wall of Fire, Yahweh, and Zealous for you.[9] And so much more!

His name is a weapon. We need to study His names and to get them deep in our spirit so we can pull them out at the right times and win the battle. We need to be warring princesses, who pull out their husband's credit card with the famous name and use it to get what is rightfully ours!

Unveiling our Weapons: Lipstick

The next weapon we discover in our hope chest is a shiny new lipstick. This lipstick is applied to our lips and is representative of the confession and words of our mouth.

There is power in the words of our mouth. Our words can curse people and situations: "So also the tongue is a small part of the body, and yet it boasts of great things. Behold, how great a forest is set aflame by such a small fire! And the tongue is a fire, the very world of iniquity; the tongue is set among our members as that which defiles the entire body, and sets on fire the course of our life, and is set on fire by hell . . . But no one can tame the tongue; it is a restless evil and full of deathly poison. With it we bless our Lord and Father; and with it we curse men, who have been made in the likeness of God" (James 3:5-9 NASB).

There may be negative confessions and positive confessions that we make every day with our mouth. Negative confessions align themselves with our flesh and the world. They are incorrect thought patterns spoken out loud that can set in motion disastrous results. Positive confessions are those that line up with the Word of God and bring about victory in the spirit and natural realm.

The story from Mark 5:25-34 is a powerful example of the power of our words. In the passage, this woman had the same physical problem for twelve years. She had been to many doctors but could find no cure or relief. This woman could have told herself that she would never be healed, that she would always suffer with this aliment, and there was no point in even venturing out into the streets and through the crowd to try to get a glimpse of this Jesus. Thankfully, she did just the contrary. Verse 28 (AMP) says, "For she kept saying, If I only touch His garments, I shall be restored to health." Did you notice what the Word says? "She kept saying," meaning she was declaring what the Lord was going to do for her, instead of repeating the problem and wallowing in self-pity and self-imposed word curses. She declared her healing, refused to speak negatively, and she received a miracle. We need to start talking to our circumstances instead of talking about them.

Confessions from our mouth that line up with the Word of God (instead of declaring the opposite) release faith and obedience in our lives. Indeed, "Life and death are in the power of the tongue, and they who indulge in it shall eat the fruit of it" (Proverbs 18:21 AMP).

"Like apples of gold in settings of silver is a word spoken in the right circumstances" (Proverbs 25:11 NASB). The Hebrew word for spoken is *dabar*, which means to be wooed. I want to woo the Lord with the life-proclaiming, love-declaring, enemy-stomping words of my mouth.

We need to hurl the Word of God at our problems and circumstances like David slung the stone at Goliath. He wants His princesses to be able to use their weapons skillfully and wisely. We are to boldly proclaim His will into the atmosphere. No longer will we despondently repeat everything negative that has ever happened to us, but we will prophesy what He will accomplish through us in the present and future.

Unveiling our Weapons: Battle Clothes

As we peer even deeper into our hope chest, we pull out a helmet and sword which is representative of our spiritual armor. The Lord has given us this wonderful protection to wear daily but so many times we waltz onto the battle field and face our opponent wearing little more than a flimsy dress. What soldier would go to the front lines in his civilian clothes? We need to daily put on the armor of God. Ephesians 6:13-17 talks of our spiritual armor that we wear daily.

We start by putting on our belt of truth. Historically the belt was a leather apron that protected the lower body. Soldiers would tuck their tunic into it so that they could run and fight and it would also hold their sheath for their sword. The Lord wants us to put on the belt of truth so that we can gird our mind with truth. The battlefield is in our mind and we need to know how to counter attack the enemy's lies with the truth of God's Word.

We then put on the breastplate of righteousness. This piece of equipment covered and protected the vital organs such as the heart, lungs, liver, and stomach. It could extend from the base of the neck to the upper part of the thighs. This is like wearing a modern bullet-proof vest, where one can walk with confidence knowing they are protected. We have righteousness given to us by His grace and it is with this God-given righteousness that we use the breastplate to repel the enemy's missiles.

We would not leave home without our shoes. It would be ludicrous to have bare feet as we go to work or shopping or to school. Likewise, this is an important part of our armor—the feet of peace. Isaiah 52:7 (NIV) says, "beautiful on the mountains are the feet of those who bring good news." Wherever we walk, we carry the peace, reconciliation, healing, and authority of the Lord. We need to realize that truth as our feet carry us about our daily activities.

The next piece of armor is the helmet of salvation that protects our mind and thought life. A powerful woman of God once illustrated for me that I should imagine the helmet of salvation filled with the blood of Jesus and as I tip it over to put it on, the blood of Jesus courses down my head and cleanses my mind. I have prayed this over many people, including myself, and it is a powerful image. The helmet protects our head and guards our minds. It is essential.

The shield of faith is a vital piece of our armor. Shield is taken originally from the root word for door because it is shaped like a door. Often it went down to the knee and covered the entire body. Some estimate it at four feet long and two feet wide. What a wonderful visual image we can have when we have our shield up! Tradition says that soldiers often oiled their shields and when faced into the sun would reflect the bright light into the enemy's eyes. We need to be daily clothed in faith so we can believe what the Word says to us and about us.

The sword of the spirit is a defensive weapon but also the only offensive weapon in the armor of God. It is only effective when the rest of the armor is in place. It is a powerful weapon of our warfare.

The Word of the Lord comes in the written Word. It goes into your spirit when you read it, then is spoken out of your mouth to combat the enemy. It is a two-edged sword. God speaks to us, and then we speak to the enemy. It is important that we are very familiar with the Word of God so that Holy Spirit can draw from this well of knowledge during battle.

Don your battle clothes daily, Warrior Princess. God has chosen you as His champion, and equipped you brilliantly for this task!

Unveiling our Weapons: The Cell Phone and the Dinner Plate

The next items we pull from our hope chest are a cell phone and an empty dinner plate. They represent the weapons that are prayer and fasting.

Prayer is conversing with our King and receiving the battle plan and instructions for maneuvers. Communicating with the Lord is like filling our gas tank up with fuel for energy to keep us going, and storing oil so our lamps can keep burning. We cannot win the battle or even go into battle in our own strength, but rather receive strategy and power through prayer.

> *"The effective prayer of a righteous man can accomplish much."*
> *(James 5:16 NASB)*

When we talk to Him it massages His heart. He loves us, desires dialogue, and wants us to have what we need. In the same way we want to equip our children so they have tools they need for school. We would not deny them pencils, glue, markers, and the whole list of supplies elementary school children are required to purchase before each new year of school. We give these gifts to our children because we want them to succeed.

"If you then, being evil, know how to give good gifts to your children, how much more shall your Father who is in heaven give what is good to those who ask Him" (Matthew 7:11 NIV). His gifts are good, indeed!

We ask Him for battle strategy and He gives it to us. But sometimes we need a bit of turbo boost to win the war. The other day I was watching my sons play a basketball video game and I noticed that one of the players would turn into fire whenever the ball was passed to him. Evidently, he was in turbo mode. He would shoot the ball and, every time he was on fire, assuredly score a point. He would never miss. The people in the stands would cheer and a special song would be played.

This is what I think fasting does for us. Fasting somehow puts us into turbo drive. We operate in turbo charge and we win against our opponent. Jesus suggested fasting to His disciples when they complained that some demons could not be driven out (Mark 9:28-29 NIV). He replied, "This kind can come out only by prayer and fasting."

Fasting and prayer intensifies our desires for our Captain's ways. Jesus taught that blessed are those who hunger and thirst after righteousness for they shall be filled. Fasting and prayer liberates us to do "greater things than these" (John 14:12 NIV).

Fasting and prayer releases greater anointing so His glory and fragrance can rest on our words and actions. Fasting and prayer sharpens the edges of our sword so we can plunge it without resistance into the throat of the enemy.

Unveiling our Weapons: Music Box Dancer

The last weapon that we will pull out is an exquisite music box. We lift the lid and hear a beautiful song of praise to the Lord as we watch a little dancer with arms raised in adoration spin around. This music box represents the powerful weapon of praise.

Praise is a weapon of warfare. Praise and worship allow us to rise above our circumstances, and render the enemy inactive in his plans to wreak havoc in our lives.

Praise affects our emotions, our thought patterns, our circumstances, and as we sow praise into the atmosphere, we are prophesying what God wants to and will do.

King Jehoshaphat instructed the singers to go before the army in battle singing praises to God. It was a divine strategy for victory. 2 Chronicles 20:21-25 (NASB) says:

> When [Jehoshaphat] had consulted with the people, he appointed those who sang to the Lord and those who praised Him in holy attire, as they went out before the army and said, "Give thanks to the Lord, for His lovingkindness is everlasting." When they began singing and praising, the Lord set ambushes against the sons of Ammon, Moab, and Mount Seir, who had come against Judah; so they were [smitten]. For the sons of Ammon and Moab rose up against the inhabitants of Mount Seir destroying them completely, and when they had finished with the inhabitants of Seir, they helped to destroy one another.

When Judah came to the lookout of the wilderness, they looked toward the multitude, and behold, they were corpses lying on the ground, and no one had escaped. And when Jehospaphat and his people came to take their spoil, they found much among them, including goods, garments, and valuable things which they took for themselves, more than they could carry. And they were three days taking the spoil because there was so much.

Praising God is a battle strategy. The enemy does not want to stick around while the high praises of God are lifted up. "Let the

Godly ones exalt in glory; let them sing for joy on their beds. Let the high praises of God be in their mouth, and a two-edged sword in their hand" (Psalm 149:5-6 NASB).

Your praises can change the atmosphere—over your household, over your workplace, over your school, and over your neighborhood. Your voice is a powerful weapon of warfare. When you declare the goodness of God and your adoration of Him, it charges the atmosphere with prophetic truth, the enemy must flee, and the Lord's provision is set in motion. The praises of our mouths catapult us from the natural into the supernatural. We are to be seated with Him in the heavenly places with Christ Jesus (Ephesians 2:6 NIV) and when we look above our circumstances and praise the Lord we are in agreement with Him.

And There's More

These weapons that we have pulled out of our hope chest are not all that our arsenal contains. Dig deeper into Him and His Word to discover the other weapons He has entrusted to you.

Guard Your Boundary

Our dowry includes weapons He has given us to defeat the enemy in all aspects of our lives and the lives of those in our sphere of influence. In Genesis, He gave Adam and Eve the instruction to guard and keep everything that He had placed in the Garden. It was Adam's responsibility to replenish, subdue, have dominion over, dress, and keep everything within his boundary. We are to do just that with everything that He has entrusted to us. "The Lord is a boundary setter and He has placed us in a boundary or personal property line that marks those things for which we are responsible."[10] A preacher once relayed that sometimes there is a war to get into the boundaries of our promises. We need to be His warring women who guard and keep everything within their sphere of influence. We are called then to multiply the kingdom by treading down the enemy and taking back our rightful inheritance.

We are His lovesick girls who love to gaze on His face and eat honey from His hand, yet we need to be quick to spring into action if there is something amiss on our watch. Isaiah 62 talks of watchmen on the walls that guard the palace from an approaching threat. Likewise, it is our position within the palace walls, in the bridal chamber which affords us a vantage point to watch for an incoming enemy. It is in our place of intimacy that we draw our energy and power and it is out of the place of intimacy we war with the weapons He has given us. We are not to be running around swinging swords and shouting foolish gibberish, but when we are

> "And as the bridegroom rejoices over the bride, so your God will rejoice over you. On your walls, O Jerusalem, I have appointed watchmen; all day and all night they will never keep silent."
> (Isaiah 62:5-6 NASB)

fully equipped and energized by His kisses then we are a force to be reckoned with. Is the enemy amused by you or afraid of you?

We are His Warrior Princesses, fully equipped for every battle. We need to be abandoned to the Captain of the Mighty Host of Heaven. Let us pledge our allegiance to Him for the Kingdom of God is at hand. Let us rise from our complacency, Warrior Princesses, and declare to the world who our Lover is and take back everything the enemy has stolen. It is our inheritance. He has given us this beautiful hope chest full of spectacular weapons. Let's put them to good use.

Prayer:

Lord I receive all the weapons You have gifted me with. I want to learn to use them and be comfortable pulling them out whenever I have need. You have crafted me so incredibly and You desire me to be fully activated to be all You dreamed I would be. I am not helpless, or incapacitated but I am equipped, able and capable to utilize every tool and weapon You have placed at my disposal. Teach me, Holy Spirit, about each weapon. Give me dreams and visions even while I sleep to enrich my understanding of how and when to use these weapons. I am yours, I am willing, and I move forward into all You have for me to be victorious in You! Amen.

Activation:

Close your eyes and imagine a large hope chest in front of you. Lift the lid and peer in to find all the weapons we talked about. Imagine you reach your hand inside and pull out a beautiful ornate cup which represents the Blood of Jesus. Think about what His Blood did for you. Next you pull out a scroll. Take the ribbon off the scroll and unfurl it to see the Names of God. His Names cover and protect us. Think about some of your favorite names of God. Next is a tube of lipstick. Take off the cap and imagine putting some of the lipstick on. We are reminded our words are so important and carry such power. Next imagine pulling out our battle clothes. First is the helmet, put it on your head. Then the sword, the belt of Truth, breastplate of righteousness, and shoes of the gospel of peace. You are fully dressed! You reach your hand in again and out comes a cell phone and empty plate which represent prayer and fasting. Pause and ask the Lord to speak to you about how these are weapons are so powerful. Lastly there is one more item in the bottom of the chest. It is a music box. Open the lid and hear the sound of musical praise and worship which rises like incense before Him. He loves when you worship Him. Pause for a few minutes and listen to what the Lord wants to say to you about all the items in the hope chest. Journal what He is saying.

Huddle Questions:

1. We war out of a place of intimacy with Jesus. How can we rest and war at the same time?

2. The weapons of our warfare (His blood, His name, our confessions, armor of God, prayer and fasting, praise) are all things that we know about; yet, so often when calamity comes, we simply wring our hands in despair and don't use this arsenal. What strategies can we take away from this to apply to our next battle?

3. How does the concept of Jesus giving us a full hope chest confuse our thinking that God has to get us out of any mess we're in?

4. What part do positive and negative confessions play in winning the battle?

Girls with Gumption: Harriet Tubman

Harriet Tubman always knew what to pack for the journey. In 1852 when she was 30, she travelled the Underground Railroad as slave and victoriously stepped over the Pennsylvania state line to freedom. The Underground Railway she travelled consisted of safe houses and secret routes run by anti-slavery sympathizers which would aid slaves on their dangerous journey to freedom. She would later write that she looked down at her hands to see if she was the same person now she had stepped into freedom. She recounted she sensed such a glory through the trees and over the fields, she felt like she was in Heaven. Born into an enslaved family, she was finally a free woman.

It was Harriot's faith which led her to have compassion toward those still enslaved, and holy outrage for the prejudice which held them captive. She wanted to help others enjoy the same freedom she experienced. Harriet's first excursion as an Underground Railway guide was courageously whisking her sister, brother in law, and their children to freedom. Friends warned her not to make the perilous trip to rescue her family, but she adamantly felt God was with her and would protect her. This was the first of nineteen trips she would make, rescuing over 300 slaves during her lifetime. She carried a pistol tucked into the waistband of her long skirt which she threatened to use if anyone tried to turn back. She knew the fate which would await runaway slaves. Although there was a $40,000 bounty for her capture, she had a fearlessness and was not afraid of what man could do to her as her trust and faith was in the Lord.

Harriet constantly talked to God and would hear what to do and where to go, ensuring safety for herself and all entrusted to her. Harriet leaned on the Lord and not her own strength, listening and obeying His Voice. She told others, "I don't know where to go or what to do, but I expect Him to lead me. And He always did!" This Warrior Princess is remembered for the courage, pluck, strength, tenacity, and wisdom the Lord equipped her with, enabling many to experience freedom and liberty.

8

Book of Destiny

"You thought you were going to be made into a decent little cottage, but He is building a palace He intends to come and live in it Himself."

– C.S. Lewis

"You will also be considered a crown of glory and splendor in the hand of the Lord, and a royal diadem (exceedingly beautiful) in the hand of your God."
(Isaiah 62:3 AMP)

When my daughter was a little girl, she very much wanted an American Girl Doll. These dolls depict girls aged eight to twelve from all over the world. There is Kaya, who is a Native American doll from the Nez Perez tribe; Josephina, who is a Mexican doll from New Mexico; Cecile, who is an African American doll from New Orleans . . . You get the picture. I can remember pouring over the catalogue with my daughter trying to choose from the many dolls. You can even customize a doll to look just like you. In the end, my daughter chose Nellie, the Irish doll, because they both have red hair. The thing that I found fascinating about this collection of dolls was that each one came with a story book. Through the pages of that book, the dolls came alive as little girls learned what era their dolls were from, what type of family they were born into, and what talents and gifts their dolls possessed. These books outlined what their doll's life was like, what part of the world they were born in, and how that affected their story.

What if we came with a storybook that detailed if our hair is straight or curly, what color eyes we have, what strengths, talents, and gifts we possess? If we loved the company of others, or preferred to be alone? If we would be a good listener, or a fantastic dancer, or we would adore chocolate, coffee, or ice cream? What if there was a book written all about us, even before we were born? It would be a Book of Destiny we could be sent home from the hospital with; like a story book instruction manual about who we would be! Psalm 139:16 (TPT) says, "You saw who You created me to be before I became me! Before I'd ever seen the light of day, the number of days You planned for me were already recorded in Your book." The Amplified Bible says, "Your eyes have seen my unformed substance; and in Your book were all written the days that were appointed for me, when as yet there was not one of them."

Wow, let that sink in a moment; He had a dream of who we would be, even before He created us. We are walking, talking creations lovingly crafted by the Master Artisan who also created the Milky Way and galaxies upon galaxies. It was He who painted the sky with the northern lights and invented the exquisiteness of snow peaked mountains and the salty spray of the ocean. This is Who wrote our Book of Destiny, all about who we are, what era of time we would be born into, what part of the earth, and how He has crafted us with everything we would need to walk out our life stories with grace and gumption.

That is a book I want to read! Paul says in Ephesians 2:10 (TPT), "We have become His poetry, a recreated people that will fulfill the destiny He has given each of us, for we are joined to Jesus, the Anointed One. Even before we were born, God planned in advance our destiny and the good works we would do to fulfill it." He says we are poetry. Smile. I receive that. Psalm 40:6-7 (TPT) states to God, "It's not sacrifices that really move your heart. Burnt offerings, sin offerings—that's not what brings You joy. But when You open my ears and speak deeply to me, I become Your willing servant, Your prisoner of love for life. So I said, 'Here I am! I'm coming to You as a sacrifice, *for in the prophetic scrolls of your book You have written about me.*'" Just in case we didn't understand the whole "for in the prophetic scrolls of your book You have written about me" thing, it is stated again in Hebrews 10:5-7.

Jeremiah 29:11 (NIV) says, "'For I know the plans I have for you,' declares the Lord, 'plans to prosper you and not to harm you, plans to give you a hope and a future.'" Just let those words wash over you, wash away all doubts and fears about the future and what you are supposed to be doing. When I researched the word "plans" in that verse, it means a cunning invention, an artistic work, imaginations and dreams. He has dreams for us which He wants us to know and understand. We each have a Scroll or Book in which is written all the plans, dreams and desires the Lord has for each one of us.

Psalm 139:16 (NLT) says: "You saw me before I was born. Every day of my life was recorded in your book, every moment was laid out before a single day had passed." When I ponder that verse, I have to ask, if He saw me before I was born, what was I doing? Was I hanging out with God, chatting about how excited I was to be all He created me to be? Were my family- and friends-to-be talking amongst ourselves in the Heavenlies about how amazing it was to finally be born and start fulfilling our Destiny Scroll? Curious ones want to know!

These verses tell us that He fashioned a scroll. He thoughtfully dreamed up who we would be and wrote it in the story of us. That Book of Destiny contains everything we are. It is the essence or identity that God sees in us. It tells the story of who we are as Heaven perceives us. I often live out my days with such a low opinion of what I am capable of. Are we living out of Heaven's identity? If only we would recall how God sees us when we wake up every day, and live our days out of that identity! How different would our lives be. That is how I want to live my life. That is how I want to respond to my trying circumstances—out of the sum of what is written in my Book of Destiny.

Your Storybook of Destiny

I remember my daughter's delight when the doll she had chosen came to our home. She tore into the package and lovingly cradled the box that contained Nellie. Peering through the plastic window we saw Nellie beaming back at us patiently waiting to meet us. We carefully lifted the lid off and there she was in all her glory, compete with her story book on top. The first thing we reached for was that book. Could it be that God tucked our Book in with us as He fashioned us in our mother's womb? He wrote in our Book the reality of who we are, what we would do in and for Him and He lovingly waits for us to ask to read our Destiny Scroll. How it must delight His heart when His children ask "Papa, what did You dream about me and wrote in my Book?" On our precious Scroll are the thoughts God has about us, who we will be and what we will be like. Have the sorrows and circumstances of life gotten us off-course and we have detoured from what is written in our Book? Allow Him to recalibrate us back from living out of the pages of what we think others think we should do to living joyfully out of what He says about us. Ask Him to help you remember what He said about you.

He had nine months alone with us, fashioning us cell by cell as He breathed into us the reality of who we would be. However, we are a product of our earthly parents and ancestral lineage as well. Scientifically, you probably learned about DNA in school. Our DNA is from our mother and father's genes, so obviously we physically carry the record of their DNA in our own. But we also have their spiritual DNA—their blessings and sins. Romans 3:23 (NASB) reminds us we all have sinned and fallen short of the glory of God. This spiritual DNA can be both a blessing and a curse. It can give you great strength from your lineage, allowing you to pursue what our Heavenly Father created you to be. But it can also hinder you in that pursuit.

Thankfully, we have our Heavenly Father's record in our Destiny Scroll of who we really are to guide us through that struggle. Depending on your family, we may need to do some housecleaning to purify and break agreement with some of the tendencies, and iniquities that do not resonate with what is written in our Book of Destiny. Allow Him to steer you in the right direction and sweep your generational lineage to ready it for the generations to come through you which will bring lovesick friends of God who will change the world around them. Regardless of our birth and origin, regardless of the iniquity patterns that came from our mother and our father's generational line, He wrapped that Scroll of who we are inside us. When we give ourselves to Him and dedicate our hearts and lives to Him and walk out being that new creation Paul talks of in 2 Corinthians 5:17, He begins to unwrap that Destiny Scroll of who we really are and we step into agreement with how Heaven sees us.

Our Heavenly Father's DNA is written in our Book. It contains the thoughts God thinks about us: who we are, who we are becoming, what we will be like. When we get an understanding of what our Scroll says, and what He has said about us, it will transform the way we think about ourselves. It will transform our faith and hope to be able to walk out what God says about us. It can only be life transforming to know how God thinks about us. I guarantee no one thinks 100% about themselves as Father thinks about us. I want to step into that reality of how Heaven sees me and begin to walk and talk it out and think in agreement with that identity. I want to unwrap the reality of who He dreamed I would be and have it emanate from me in everything I do and to everyone I interact with.

Could it be God's light, sound and fragrance is diffused through us when we are living in the reality of who we are in Him? 2 Corinthians 2:15 says that we are the perfume of life. We are made in our Father's image and when you consider how incredible He is, and we carry His DNA, how can we think poorly of ourselves? How can we not appreciate the way He created us to be? Embrace the uniqueness and beauty He has placed inside you and say yes to what He dreamed you would be, even if right now you can only see a fraction of a glimmer of who that is.

Living in His Destiny for us

When we give our lives to the Lord, we become a new creation and we have access to all of Heaven's bounty. By living out of this new identity, we are granted access to our Scroll. He gives us the desires of our heart and that Scroll becomes our testimony as we seek to discover what is written on it. It is like a beautiful gift He presents to us and it is our delight to unwrap the box and unravel the Scroll and begin to live out of the testimony of what He's written about you. We only need to ask Him to unwrap our Book of Destiny so we can begin to live out of Heaven's reality of who we are.

I love giving gifts and I am terrible at waiting to give those gifts. I'll buy Christmas gifts for everyone and then I'll tell my kids what I got for the other kids. I'm so excited I don't even want to open my gifts but just watch everyone else unwrap theirs! What happens when you give a beautifully wrapped gift to someone? They unwrap it! Sometimes someone may carefully pick away at the tape until they can cautiously free the wrapping from the gift. Some save the wrapping to be used again. Others joyously tear away, eager to expose the gift that lies temporarily hidden. It is that simple. Tear away the wrapping and discover your Book. If I can't wait to give my kids their Christmas gifts, how much

> *Tear the wrapping paper off the gift of who you are and begin to walk in the fullness of your Heaven-identity.*

more does the Father say "I can't wait for you to unwrap what I truly think of you, I can't wait until you begin to walk into what I've created for you!" If it gives us that much pleasure to give gifts, what does it do for Father God Who walks in the perfectness of Who He is to be so proud of us and delighted in us as we begin to live this Heaven-identity out. I want to begin to unwrap the wrapping paper off the gift of who I am and begin to walk in the fullness of what that is. When we step into who we were created to be it is His delight to have all of Heaven come into agreement with His creation!

Discovering the contents of your Destiny Scroll

I have a friend who is an adventurer. Literally. Her Facebook page is full of exotic places she goes (Africa, Malaysia, Borneo, mostly places with lots of bugs), disarmingly fearless things she attempts (Deep sea diving, hang gliding, climbing in Nepal, posing with large bugs), and a joy of life she exudes (many pictures of very large, fascinating bugs). Part of what is written in her Book is a fearless exploration of places others have no desire to go, and the Lord has used her to bring His good news to those places where others only read about in the news. That is who she is, and I love her for that. God loves her for that, and *made* her for that!

What did the Lord make you for? Ask the Lord to begin to reveal to you all that He dreamed about you before He knit you in your mother's womb. If you asked your family and a few close friends, "What are the words you would use to describe me?," you would probably receive the same words over and over. The redemptiveness of those qualities are, in part, what is written in our Book. For example, if people repeatedly say, you are a good listener and that is a quality you are known for, that is part of the unique design God wove into you. That is part of the God-given identity of who you are.

You may have received a prophetic word of encouragement from someone. They are reading out of your Book, whether they know that or not. They are simply repeating what the Lord is saying about you and highlighting those qualities. They are repeating how Heaven sees you. Listen for those whispers and shouts the Lord puts in your everyday life of how He sees you. They may be in the grateful words of a child, or in a meaningful talk with a friend, or a prophetic word from a prophet.

Sometimes we may have done things that are written in our

Book, without ever reading it. I remember when I was choosing a major for college, I chose journalism because I loved to get to the bottom of how things worked, and I loved words and reading. It made sense to me, at the time. The further I delved into journalism classes, the more I disliked it. I remember being asked in an assignment to interview someone and extract an angle out which would expose that person. I did not want to do that. This was not how I was wired. As I sat with the Lord (more like complained to Him), He asked me what I enjoyed doing the most? The more I thought about it, I realized I had always taught—summer camp, swimming lessons, violin lessons, Sunday School. Even as a little girl I would sit my younger brother and sister down on little plastic chairs, stand in front of them, and "teach" them. I would draw up work sheets for them to complete and then I would grade it. How they must have rolled their eyes when I gave them back their papers with my big red checkmarks. It dawned on me that my whole life, the thing I loved doing most was coming alongside someone else and helping them understand and learn. I switched my major to teaching and never looked back. That is who I am. I even have a mug that says "I'm a Teacher, what's your super power?" I ended up teaching high school for years, as I felt that was my mission field. I was operating out of what was written in my Book and it brought me such joy. There is always a divine pleasure that comes out of operating in our God-dreamed capacity.

What are things you do that energize you and bring you joy? When you are operating out of those activities you are living out of your Book of Destiny. There can be times in our life where we are not living out of our Book and could be stuck in a job we detest, involved in a toxic relationship, or a in difficult family situation. Sometimes we may look around and see someone living out of their Book of Destiny and it looks pretty amazing, for them. For you, not so much, as you consider the trajectory your life may have taken. Comparison is a dangerous game to play, and one that the Lord never authorized when we look with jealousy or envy at the gifts and talents of others. Please understand, no one else can fulfill your Book of Destiny. No one else can pick up your Book and live out of it. We need to stop side-eying one another and comparing ourselves to others seeming fantastical giftings or outstanding talents, or over the top abilities. Just. Be. You. Thankfully, God does not require or expect us to live out of someone else's Book. Now we need to just figure out and live out of what is written in ours!

Can't find your Scroll?

What if you feel you've missed it, and made choices that were contrary to God's best for you? What if you've felt you've wasted your years, or your dreams have not been fulfilled? The good news is, God redeems time! In 2 Peter 3:8-9 (NASB), He tells us that "with the Lord, one day is as a thousand years, and a thousand years as one day. The Lord is not slow to fulfill His promise as some count slowness." The Lord can supernaturally restore lost years, unfulfilled dreams, and lost inheritance. Joel 2:25 (KJV) says, "I will restore to you the years that the swarming locust has eaten." The Lord can restore any plans you feel you may have missed as you took twisty detours and wrong turns in His plan for your life. Paul in Philippians 3:13-14 (BSB) reminds us to forget what is behind and strain toward what is ahead, press on toward the goal to win the prize of God's Heavenly calling in Christ Jesus. Repeat after me: "This is my time of purpose and alignment. I decree I am fulfilling those things written on my Destiny Scroll, written in my Book of Destiny. I declare God is accelerating me and redeeming the time and dreams that were lost." Amen!

What to do with your Heaven-identity

So now that you have asked the Lord for a peek inside your Scroll, and you are determining how to live out of that, what is the next step? Like the American Girl Doll book for each doll which gives a concise paragraph about who that girl is, we can write our own paragraph of who God sees when He looks at us. We each need an identity statement that we can live out of, which reminds us of who we are when we are in a tough circumstance, or when the world tells us we are not worthy or not enough. We need to read that identity statement when life makes us so weary we feel we cannot go on. We need to remember that we can do all things in His strength. When we craft this statement, we can read it out loud over ourselves and allow it to get into our souls and become part of our DNA. Sometimes we just need a reminder of who we are.

I met a lady last year who loves to pan for gold. She purposely travels places to check out creeks, streams and rivers for gold. Armed with a portable shallow gold pan, she eagerly tips the pan into the water and swirls the silt around and around, holding the pan up to the warmth of the sun and watching for the glint of a shimmer of gold. Over the years she has found some sizable nuggets of gold and those trophies sit in a clear locket she wears around her neck. She is a panner of gold. When we are assembling our identity statements, it is like panning for gold. We are swirling the pan, looking at past and present words of encouragement spoken over us. Our statement becomes refined the more time we seek out what He is saying about us, then they become who we are that we can proudly wear like our comfortable go-to jeans that fit us just right.

To start writing out our identity statement, assemble your journals, scraps of paper, anything where you may have jotted down encouraging words someone spoke over you. I have a friend who has a "Joy Box" and in it she places all the birthday cards, thank you notes and encouraging words others have written to her and said about her. If you have a place you have put those type of cards, get that out. Sift through your old journals, and current ones with sentences you may have written down about what the Lord was saying about who you are. Writing an identity statement may take a bit of commitment, but it is so worth it. The Lord is always speaking to us about our identity, we just need to tune in to His Voice! Think about those things you are good at, that really energize you instead of draining you. Maybe you are an amazing encourager, or listener, or you know just what someone needs and can make that happen. Look at any gifts or strengths you have, or personality tests you may have done. What speaks to you when you look at the results? You may be able to point back to major prophetic words you received, or a defining moment when you realize a special strength that you possess. What is your go-to scripture verse or life verse? Look it up in different translations. Is there a God encounter in your word? Take all of those words and begin to compile "I am" statements. They may be "I am a seeker and discoverer of God's hidden treasures," or, "I am an atmosphere changer," or "I am an Esther who possesses the wisdom to know what to do in challenging circumstances." You get the picture. It is the Father's good pleasure to reveal to you who you are in Him. This is your inheritance. When we know how we are wired and what strengths and gifts we walk in, we can live out of the fullness of these inheritance words. We walk and live out of how God sees and treats us!

Heaven sees you as fully whole, fully compete, fully in Him. This is the identity we are to intercede out of, act out of, make decisions out of, worship out of, live out of. Declare these statements over yourself until God's reality become your reality. This is already how God sees you. It is the Father's good pleasure to reveal to you who you are in Him. What is written in our book is how we are known in Heaven. It is our persona. When He declares your persona, He is saying this is what I am making in you and He needs everything in your life to come into alignment with that identity. He needs your own negativity about yourself, and your world to come into alignment with what is written in your book.

Speak your identity statement over yourself, write it out and place it somewhere to remind you who you are. Rest in knowing that you do not have to be someone you are not. You do not have to do everything others ask you to do if it does not line up with your destiny and identity. Breathe deep and let the Lord speak into your spirit the Truth of how Heaven sees you. Live out of that reality. You are incredible!

> *Write down your identity statement and put it where you see it, everyday.*

Like the American Girl Doll Book who tells starry eyed little girls all the wonders of their valued dolls, you too can read aloud to the atmosphere around you who you are. Circumstances must bend to accommodate His daughters who walk in their identity and destinies.

Prayer:

Father today I come into agreement with the Book of Destiny which You have written about me. I come into agreement with the things that You wrote about my life, the things that I would walk in and the things that no one can do but me.

I open my heart to You and in my heart and I unravel the testimony of the Book You wrote for me. I am going to walk out my Kingdom identity that will be displayed around me in signs and wonders. I am known in Heaven as a friend of God. Today I open the testimony of my Book and ask that You would release out of Heaven the agreement that I will become what You have written. I receive your acceptance. You are pleased with me.

I seal within my life the testimony of Jesus, by faith, and today I open my heart and I walk and live out of who you created me to be. I come into agreement with You; let my heart be revealed in Your image. Amen.

Activation and Huddle Questions:

We are going to take some time to craft an identity statement based on our Destiny Scroll. This identity statement can be a few sentences or paragraphs long. This may take time, like weeks and even months to fine tune it, but let's get started now.

Allow yourself to see yourself as God sees you. Soon you will have an identity statement you can proclaim into the atmosphere whenever circumstances or life causes you to forget who you truly are. Rise up, see yourself and live out of how you are known by God!

1. Look for inheritance words. How would your best friend describe you? What are you good at doing? (encouraging, listening, serving)

2. What are major prophetic words you've received over your lifetime? Look for key words and phrases, promises, and conditions.

3. What are you passionate about? What gets you out of bed in the morning, or gets you excited to know you are going to be doing something that day?

4. What is your go-to scripture or life verse? Look it up in different translations. Is there encounter in your word?

5. Gather up all your observations and begin to form simple sentences about your identity. Compile "I am" statements. Here are some examples:

  · I am a seeker and discoverer of God's hidden treasures.

  · I am an atmosphere changer.

  · I am a faith filled presence carrying warrior resting peacefully under His wings. I am prepared by Holy Spirit to launch out into battle.

  · I am an Esther who possesses a love, purity, favor, and

wisdom. I am a beloved daughter who has the joy of the Lord as my strength.

Choose a sentence or two from what you have composed in your identity statement and say it out loud to the group. This is a powerful way to begin to proclaim to the atmosphere who you are in Him! Encourage one another with your statements!

Girls with Gumption: Heidi Baker

Heidi Baker has witnessed miracles. Once a friend brought Heidi's family of four dinner; but, Heidi also needed to feed about 100 orphans she was caring for. The dinner was multiplied and every child was fed. She says, "the heart of the Father is loving the fatherless," and she lives this motto daily by reaching the poorest of the poor in Mozambique. Heidi searches for orphaned children in the streets, gutters, garbage dumps, and under bridges, bringing them home with her where they learn what it means to be loved and part of the family of God.

A self-proclaimed "laid down lover of God," she ministers to the poor and orphaned in Mozambique through their ministry Iris Global, where she and her husband Rolland radiate the light and love of Jesus. Initially given a dilapidated orphanage in Maputo with 320 hungry children, Heidi leaned on the Lord for provision. Later shut down by the government for teaching the children about the Lord, the Bakers found land in a nearby city and built an orphanage, dorms, and even a bible college. A network of thousands of churches and church-based orphan care sparked by Heidi and Rolland in all ten provinces of Mozambique provides discipling and hope to many by welcoming the love of Jesus and power of Holy Spirit.

Through threat of death, disease, cyclones, floods, and many other perils, Heidi sees daily miracles manifest in every area of need. Her love for Jesus shines in her countenance and often renders her unable to articulate. A favorite speaker at conferences around the world, Heidi is so full of Jesus she often will release the Presence of the Lord in a meeting and not be able to teach as the audience is lost in the revelation of the Beauty of the Lord. People Heidi prays for receive salvation, healing, and miracles daily. Dead are raised back to life as Heidi holds their bodies and loves on them. Her desire is to take in a million orphaned children in her lifetime, and she is well on her way towards that goal. Heidi's daily prayer is, "Lord pick me up like a paintbrush and paint Your picture." This Warrior Princess is a human diffuser of the fragrance of Jesus as she cares for the poorest of the poor and brings the love of the Father to the orphaned and forgotten.

9

What Is Our Identity?

"You are a paintbrush in the hands of an Artist."

– Heidi Baker

> The Lord gives the command; the women who proclaim the good tidings are a great host: Kings of armies flee, they flee, and she who remains at home will divide the spoil!
> *(Psalm 68:11 NASB)*

Alright ladies, can I have your attention? Yes, all of you. It's been such a pleasure to spend time with you in these chapters. But there is something I want to show you. Gather around, and come with me; it's just over this hill, in the valley on the other side. No, you don't have to get dressed up—it's a "come as you are" event. Alright, follow me. You are going to be blown away. Ok, almost there . . . we are about to reach the crest of the hill. There! Can you see it? As far as the eye can see on this rolling grass, an impossibly long banquet table is lavishly set and ready for your arrival. Pick a place to sit. There is room for everyone. We all have a seat at the table.

Lean in and look closely at how each place setting is different. I see one which is a woodsy place setting with a charger of mossy green, a beautiful wooden bowl and birchbark cup. I also see an ornate china setting, with whisper thin royal blue and gold tea cup and saucer, and an achingly beautiful china plate. Oh my goodness, we all choose our assigned places. The One who flung the glittering stars against the velvet sky, the One Who holds the winds in His fist and says "Peace, Be Still" is the One who chose your place setting. It is crafted just for you. He knows you so well. He whispers to you as He pushes your chair in to the table, whispering in your ear, "You, Daughter, are fully known and loved by Me." Wow, I can feel His warm embrace and love down to my toes. Can't you?!

Soon, foods are brought out on large silver platters. The food is beautiful, abundant and exquisitely plated. We gingerly reach for unfamiliar dainties and cautiously hold them up to our lips. We laughingly encourage one another to take a bite. Soon, new flavors and tastes burst on our tongues. There are foods of colors we have never seen. Have you ever seen fruit colored brilliant turquoise? The air around us is punctuated with beautiful sounds and music. We feel His peace encapsulating us and we are in the moment—cares and worries we carried with us to the table are now a distant memory. What is this food, and that one? We instinctively know: this purple treat is the kindness of God which floods us with satisfaction, this liquid gold drink from our cups is His goodness which fills us up head to toe. On and on we try and experience new goodies from the table. "Taste and see that I am good!" He smiles. We look at one another over the plates and platters, sights and sounds and marvel in this incredible experience.

Wait, quiet down. I see Him standing at the end of the table. He wants to say something. We put down our food and turn our attention toward the head of the table, where He picks up his cup for a speech:

"My Warrior Daughters," He begins, *"I commission you this day to go out to the world I have placed you in to be My hands and feet. Be who you were created to be. Live without limits. Love without restraint. You are My emissary of justice, called to love yourself and those I have placed around you. Everything I dreamed you would be when I wrote in your Destiny Scroll is how I see you. Live out of that identity. You are loved. You are chosen. You are enough.*

"Bring your sparkle and effervescence to those who have the privilege of knowing you. Stop holding your breath, let it out and allow My Life to flood you with light. You are contagious to those around you for I am the Fragrance of love that emanates from you. You radiate with My glory and change the atmosphere of every place you enter. Lean back

and rest in Me. Do not try to do things in your own strength. Roll your cares on to Me and allow Me to carry them for you. You will find life is so much easier that way.

"*Be quick to forgive others and seek forgiveness when you are the transgressor. I do not keep records of wrongs. Live life in the freedom I paid for on the Cross. It is your inheritance, along with all the treasures of Heaven. You have access to it all. You are Loved extravagantly and wholly. You are My mouthpiece; speak out boldly what I say.*

"*Ahead of you is your finest hour, the fulfillment of your wildest dreams. I've got you, I see you, and I love you.*" He raises his glass toward us, as we all to raise our glasses in response.

"All for Your Glory Jesus!"

We all toast our cups and cheer. I don't know about you, but I will never be the same. I am ready to live and love in the light of His countenance. Wait, there's more? Each of us is presented with a necklace. Each necklace is unique and different and speaks to our individual identity and destiny. Which one did you get? Oh, a wedding ring necklace to signify your covenant with the Lord? Love that. What did you over there get? A heart necklace? To signify your changed heart towards Him? That's amazing. I got a necklace with a lion on it, the Lion of Judah. Yes, that is exactly what I've been asking for more understanding of—His protection and the fierce way I am loved by Him. He is so good.

Our banquet has ended, and it is time for us to live as His warriors in the world. Well, let's gather up our things, it's time to leave. Oh, the angels will take care of the dishes? I love this place!

Let's press pause on this incredible picture. I want to point out that this is who you are. You are in this incredible picture (right there, on the left). Do you see yourself at the table?

Let's recap what we've learned since we've started this journey together.

· You are part of an epic story which involves you as the heroine, Jesus as your Rescuer Redeemer. And, you have an enemy you must battle.

· You are ridiculously loved by Your Heavenly Father who wants you to live out of the truth that you are beautifully designed and created for purpose and destiny.

· You were made for an intimate relationship with Jesus and learn to fall in love with Him by spending time with Him and getting to know every crevice of His face.

· You can learn to let go of stinging words others have said to or about us. These can become like arrows which wound deeply if we allow them. But you learned how to become adept at catching the arrows before they even land, breaking them in half and giving them to Jesus. You can then receive His healing balm to cover and heal every wound and hurt.

· You have the ability to hear God's voice, and communicate with Him, all the time! You studied how to hear God's voice for yourself and even for others so you can give encouragement from the Lord.

· Your words are containers of power. You know how explosive it can be when you come into alignment with those words whether they are positive or negative. Your words are weapons of power which frame the atmosphere around you for the miraculous to thrive.

· You studied how important your thought life is and how to reign it in so you can keep your thoughts fixed on the Lord. You know how you can tidy up your imagination and allow for it to be a meeting place with your Savior.

· You are armed with many wonderous tools and weapons which help you walk out each day with destiny design.

· You have a Book of Destiny which is Father's delight for you to read and live out of. It is a blueprint for destiny which activates opportunity and blessing in your everyday life.

Wow, that was quite the journey! Armed with this knowledge and understanding of how incredible He created us, we can give ourselves permission to live out of this identity. We are His, we have purpose, we can live with passion. So how do we live out this identity?

Living This Identity

Well, we need to understand ourselves based on His love for us. We trade all our wrong thinking about how inadequate we are, how we do not measure up, how we are found lacking in so many areas; we gather those mindsets up and we trade them for

His Truth. I remember watching a show on TV where someone would start with a paperclip and make a series of trades. They might trade the paperclip for a clock and turn around and trade the clock for a vintage sign, and so the trades continue. What one person values might be just what someone else has no use for anymore. The episode I remember, they started with a paperclip and ended with a camper! That is an incredible trade. However, is that not what the Lord invites us to do? We trade our fears, inadequacies, doubts, failures and He give us back our true identity, value, worth, esteem, purpose, and significance. These are all fruits of our love relationship with Him. We then live out of those fruit as we learn to get comfortable in our identity as God sees us.

You have to ask yourself two things. Am I willing to let go of my old identity, woven with fears, failures, the old way of doing things, and embrace the new identity we have discovered? We also need to ask ourselves, am I willing to step into all He created for me to be? To say yes to those questions, we have to say goodbye to the old way of doing things. You cannot keep your old identity and carry your new one in your hand to be worn at a later date. That's like wearing your workout clothes and carrying your Bridal gown in your hand. You know the gown is custom made just for you, but you are not ready to get out of your old stretchy pants yet. You need to choose which one you will put on, and then walk in it.

The fact is God loves you, just as you are, but wants you to step into the fullness of all He created you to be. Everything He does and says is about Love. When we look at when love is first mentioned in the Bible, we find it in Genesis 22:2. God says to Abraham, "Take now . . . your only son, whom you love, Isaac, and go to the land of Moriah, and offer him there as a burnt offering on one of the mountains of which I tell you" (NASB). Wait a minute, so love sometimes means sacrifice? If you are serious about walking in your new identity, are you willing to sacrifice your old identity so He can give you a new one? If you are willing, this Love you are saying yes to is where all the answers to your deepest questions are found. Who am I? What is my purpose here? Our identity and destiny can only be worked out of our love relationship with the Lord. Accepting the identity He dreamed for us and living out of that identity allows us to fully express who we were created to be. We cannot help then but bring Him glory. Is that not true transformation, or metamorphosis, as mentioned in 2 Corinthians 5:17 (TPT): "Now if anyone is enfolded into Christ, he has become an entirely new person. All that is related to the old order has vanished. Behold, everything is fresh and new."

You may not feel so fresh and new currently, but there is no pain wasted in the Kingdom of God. He tells us He works all things together for our good in Romans 8:28 (NLT). Everything you have gone through He is going to redeem it to bring beauty out of the ashes of tragic circumstances which in turn releases hope to others in their times of dire need. We leave our past in the rearview mirror as we fasten our hearts to the future. We run, Divine invitation in hand, towards the victory prize of being fully encapsulated in His Love. We are changed as we align ourselves with His thoughts about us, His Words about us, and His will for our destiny in Him.

If we believe Psalm 139:16—that He knew us before we were born, and He lovingly crafted us to be who we are—then that means at one point, every part of us was open to Him. Our very DNA, every encoded sequence of our genetics, every quirky personality trait was exposed to the fire of His eyes. He is calling us into a love relationship which is transparent, vulnerable, and completely open; where we are revealed before His eyes and all barriers and protective coverings are removed. We trust Him implicitly as we abandon ourselves to Him. This is the love God is inviting us to access. We can allow every thought, emotion, memory, and experience to be open before Him so He can bring healing and realign it to conformity with who He dreamed we would be from the very beginning. Can we allow His love to penetrate the deepest recesses of our lives and engage every fiber of our being? We welcome the soothing balm of His Presence which heals all traces of trauma, pain, oppression, fear, depression, and loneliness. Before you ever sinned, God had already made provision in Jesus to bring you back to Himself. Before God asked Abraham to sacrifice his son Isaac, He sent a ram up the other side of the mountain to be the provision. He is a God wholly in love with you, before you even knew of Him!

> "You even formed every bone in my body when You created me in the secret place, carefully, skillfully shaping me from nothing to something. You saw who You created me to be before I became me! Before I'd ever seen the light of day, the number of days You planned for me were already recorded in Your book."
> (Psalm 139:15–16 TPT)

He stands in front of us, and holds out His waiting hands, ready for us to place our fears, self-sufficiency, self-preservation, and every single care onto Him. We hand those things to Him one by one and we let our Prince of Peace take them in Divine Exchange for His goodness, His peace, His boldness, His healing. We receive His gifts by faith, not by striving but by resting and trusting in Him. Sounds too easy, right?

The Enemy's Plan

The enemy attempts to steal our identity, in other words, he is the original identity thief! He is only successful if we do not understand who we are and Whose we are. The enemy lies to us about who we are, our value, and deceives us into believing lies about ourselves. We need to not allow our circumstances to define our reality for they are only temporal and passing. You are not the sickness you have, you are not the rejection you just walked through … You get the idea. We turn back to Him and allow the soothing balm of His Presence to heal all traces of trauma, oppression, fear, etc.

I once read a story of a princess long ago whose parents were assassinated when she was just a toddler. She was sent to the countryside and raised as a commoner, completely oblivious to the fact she was royalty. When she was in her twenties there was a coup who overthrew the current monarchy and she was sought out as the rightful heir to the throne. The problem was, she did not know who she was and had not been taught to think like royalty for her true identity had been hidden from her. Are we not like royalty who has been raised as a commoner? Has our identity been stolen from us by the enemy? When we repent where we have come into agreement with those lies, we detach from the ways of behaving which are not befitting of royalty because they are not attributes of the King. We then allow the beauty of His nature to flow through us, and His fragrance is diffused through us into the atmosphere. We receive our identity back and live from that place of authority and power in the secret place. We synchronize our thinking with the Lord's and guard our connections with Him. The key is through surrender to living a life of abiding in Him. This is the highest form of warfare for the Lord overshadows us and that is Who the enemy sees when he glances our way. The King goes with us wherever we go. The truth of our identity becomes the power and dignity of who we are.

A Picture of Our Identity

Okay, now back to our vision from the beginning of this chapter. Back to our seat at the table. We have just finished dinner, been celebrated by the Prince of Peace, given a gift and now we are trying to contain our excitement as we gather ourselves together to leave for the next step of our great adventure.

We walk back up the hill together, arms flung around each other, laughter punctuating the air. Hearts full, feeling satisfied and joy filled. We are the warrior daughters, the light carriers of His glory, the releasers of His fragrance wherever we boldly walk as Holy Spirit leads. We are simultaneously the sons of God and the Bride of Christ who have torn the wrapping paper off of the gift that is our identity and we walk out the identity which we are already known by in Heaven. That is who you are Warrior Daughter. Fully loved, seen, and know by Him; empowered to walk out of the blueprint He crafted for us. There is a lot of us. We are a family. We are a company of Warrior Daughters from Psalm 68:11 who are pursuing more of Jesus, more face to face time with Him, more transformational revelation from His Word, more walking with understanding of His mysteries. I love this. This is who you are. Now take my arm and let's walk it out. Let His Light within you radiate and illuminate the atmosphere around you. Daughter, you are lit from within. Now go and glow!

Prayer:

Lord, you've got me. I desire to be wholly yours. I surrender, submit and embrace all You have said about me, everything You've dreamed I would be and do, and every plan You have for me. I desire to know You better, and to fall more deeply in love with You with each passing day. I'm all in. Give me the courage and revelation I need to step into all You have said about me. Escort me into a deeper understanding of Your Word, Your Ways, and Your Love. I am Your Warrior Princess. Amen!

Activation and Huddle Questions:

Imagine Jesus standing in front of you, reaching His Hands out to you. Place your hands in His. Imagine what His face looks like, what is the expression in His eyes when He looks into your eyes? Listen for what He is saying to you now. He is embracing you in His arms. You feel His Love tangibly all around you, wrapping you up like a warm and cozy hug. Lean into Him. Tell Him everything you are thinking and feeling. Listen to what He whispers in your ear. Look up into His face again and thank Him. Ask Him to seal every word and picture He has given you in your heart. One last hug, and step back, still feeling His Love wrapped around you. Journal what you experienced.

Share with your group if you are comfortable what you saw and heard Jesus say to you. Your experience could be so encouraging to someone else. Our Testimony of encounter with the Lord draws others into a deeper revelation of His Love. If you did not experience something similar, or even felt nothing at all, that's okay. Open up your heart to Him and practice it again anytime, expectant that He wants to say something to you. The more you practice, the easier it gets to see and hear. Press into everything He wants you to experience. Finish the huddle with prayers of blessings over one another to step into all Jesus has for each of you. Your future in Him is shiny and bright!

Afterword: Dear Daughter

Hi there. Can I share something with you? It's kind of personal, but I wanted to share some closing thoughts with you, like a mother would with a daughter. Would that be ok with you?

Dear Warrior Daughter,

I have been praying for you as I've written this book. I have imagined who you are and I have been praying for your journey of reading this study. I can see you. You are such a joy to my heart. God couldn't have designed you any better. If no one has ever said this to you, let me be the one to say it. I want to tell you that you are amazing young woman who is so spontaneous, joyful, funny, affectionate, and loving. Your eyes sparkle with the light of heaven. I imagine you as "super girl"—wearing a pink, glittering cape; smiling in a confident and mischievous way; exuding inner, stubborn strength; showing plenty of silliness; and bursting with extraordinary will and creativity. You are a beautiful person inside and out. My prayer is that your inner beauty will only grow more radiant with each passing year. I pray that you will develop such a love for your Lord that you will be ruined for anything else but knowing Him. These may seem like strong words. I know that most mothers or mentors only want their children to be happy, but I want so much more for you, my friend. I want you to take your place as only you can, as the Warrior Princess God destined you to be.

I pray many things for you—that you know your story, that you fall in love with the Lord, that you can learn to catch and heal your soul-arrows, that you may hear God's voice, that you channel the power of your words, that you cultivate and hedge-in your thought-life, that you take up your God-given weapons, and that you thrive in the destiny and identity God has put before you. God has equipped you for such a time as this, and it is my prayer that you rise up and bask in the Lord's protection and battle plan. These are my last few prayers for you, Warrior Daughter.

It is my prayer you may discover for yourself that you were fashioned for intimacy. When I use the word "intimate" in relation to God, I mean a close, trusting, secret-sharing, comforting, loving, abandoned relationship with Jesus. Your Savior can be to you your Cross-dying, sin-forgiving, resurrected, life-giving, sickness-healing Best Friend. If you let Him, He can be your dragon-slaying Knight in shining armor.

It is hard to imagine having a close relationship with the God of the Universe who flung the stars in space and set galaxies spinning in their places. It is, however, true. He is smitten with you. He tells you in Psalm 139:17-18 (TPT) that His thoughts towards you are more than the grains of sand on the beach. Can you imagine standing on the shores of the ocean and trying to pick up the sand grains one by one to count them? It would be impossible, yet God tells you that He thinks about you more than those grains. He loves you, Daughter. He knit you in your own mother's womb and formed you into the beautiful woman you are becoming, and He even wrote down in a Book all the special things about you. Psalm 139:16 (KJV) says "Your eyes saw my substance, being yet unformed. And in Your book they all were written, the days fashioned for me, when as yet there were none of them." You are so loved by many in your life right now but we cannot even touch the kind of love that your Creator has for you. It is with this kind of love that He calls you to a deeper relationship with Him.

Many times, we struggle with accepting that God would even want a close relationship with us. We can get so caught up with work, school, friends, activities, and family, that God gets edged out of our day and the only contact we have with him is a quick prayer breathed during a crisis or before you eat. Sometimes we don't know how to reach out to Him and so we don't. Other times we think we have to earn His love or attention. We need to remember we can never get to the point where we think we are good enough for Him to want to spend time with us. Often we have been hurt or cast aside by friends or family that have tried to get closer to us. That rejection forms a wound in our heart and to protect ourselves we often push others away, including God, before they get too close and hurt us. I want you to know, Warrior Daughter, that although some of these things may cause you to give up in your pursuit of drawing closer to the Lord; there is so much to be gained from pressing through and opening your heart to the warmth of His incredible love for you.

You can have an intimate relationship with the Lord. James 4:8 (ESV) says, "Draw near to God and He will draw near to you." The word "draw" in that verse means to commune with God in prayer so to "accomplish the desired and cherished fellowship with Him." When you pray, you are talking one-on-One with your Heavenly Father, who has counted even the hairs on your head. He is insanely in love with you, Warrior Daughter, and wants to spend time with you. It is His delight when, even in a weak, feeble way, you communicate with Him in prayer and reach out for more of Him. You can ask Him what is on His heart and then quiet yourself to allow Him to speak back to you.

I pray that you would know and love God more each day, through prayer and time spent in His presence. Sometimes, prayer is hard work because you may not feel like talking to God but may be mad at Him for allowing things to happen in your life. Our silence only lets roots of bitterness and self-pity form in our hearts. Just like you need to talk things out when you've had a disagreement with someone, so you need to talk things out with God. Never think prayer is unnecessary or boring—it is the umbilical cord that connects you to your Heavenly Father. Without it you would be cut off from nourishment and life. Pursue this prayer thing. Get really good at it while you are young. It is the most important form of communication you will ever have.

Another way that we can cultivate intimacy with the Lord is just by spending time with Him. There are so many things that can gobble our hours each day—social media, spending time with friends, being involved in various activities, and the list goes on. These things can be good, but are they the best way to steward our time? We need to set aside time each day to get to know Him better. Some of your closest friends are your best friends because you spend so much time with them. You take classes together, work together, hang out, and text one another. You know what their likes and dislikes are. You know their favorite colors and type of foods they like to eat. You are well acquainted with them because over time you have gotten to really know them. It is the same way with God. The more time we spend in His presence, talking to Him, and listening to Him, the better we know Him.

Sometimes you can just sit in the presence of the Lord and not say anything to Him, and that is alright. There is such sweetness in being in the presence of the one you love. It is true of our relationship with God. He loves for us just to sit with Him and let Him love on us, silently.

We also get to know the Lord better by worshipping Him. When Adam and Eve walked with Him before the fall they communicated with the Lord spirit to Spirit. When we worship the Lord, we open our spirit to Him like a flower lifts its head to the sun. Worship carries us from the earthly worries into the Heavenly wonders of His Kingdom. Worship catapults us from our selfish ambitions and allows us to concentrate on Someone who not only is enamored with us but who lifts us up into His Throne room and lets us in on the conversations of Heaven. You are a worshipper. Mary of Bethany was a worshipper of God and soaked the Lord's feet with her perfumed oil and her tears. She loved to sit at His feet, spending time worshipping Him. Our worship opens a door into the things of God. We walk through that door into the deeper things. Mary discovered the "one thing" mentioned in Luke 10:42. It is my prayer that you will too.

I pray that the Word would be your foundation and joy. When my own daughter was little, she loved to look at pictures of our family vacations, baby pictures, dance recitals, sports events— these pictures told the story of our life. In some of the photos she looked mad or had just finished crying when the picture was shot. I remember one time she didn't like what she was wearing but the family didn't want to wait for her to change outfits. Other times she had more interesting things to do than stand still for a picture and so we had to be quick when taking it. These images tell a story about our family. In the same way, the Word of God is our photo album telling us the stories of the Trinity. The sons and daughters of God fill the pages and point to tales and lessons with each turned page. Study the Word. It is where you will also meet your Lord. John 1:1 tells us that Jesus is the Word. He is the living Word of God. When you devour the Word of God it becomes life. His promises, descriptions of Himself, plans for your life and hidden mysteries are all contained in its pages. Take time daily to eat from the Word, sometimes a snack and on days that allow a many course meal. You can never eat too much and will never feel full. It is through the Word of God that we glimpse new aspects of our Lord and fall even more in love with Him. Sometimes His Word is hard to understand. If we invite Holy Spirit who is our Teacher and sit in His classroom,

He begins to open the Scriptures to us in ways we've never seen them before.

The Word of God is like a colorful garden. If you hurriedly walked past it, you would see the heads of the flowers bopping in the breeze. If you slowed down and looked harder you would see the ladybugs dotting the green leaves of the flowers. However, if you stopped and sat down by the garden you would not only see the many vibrant colors of the flowers, and the different shapes and veins on the leaves, but you would see the stems that hold the plant upright, and if you dug away at the earth you would see the roots that web down into the soil. It is the same when you read the Word. The longer you are willing to read, ponder, and dig, the more you will see. I pray you will be a devourer of His Word.

Warrior Daughter, you have a long life-journey ahead of you. Sometimes the path is wide and smooth, and other times it is dark, narrow, and uphill. The most important thing that I can encourage you in this life is how to place your hand in the One who walks beside you. I want you to be intimately acquainted with your Lord. I want you to converse freely with Him in prayer, to be an abandoned worshipper, and to be a lover of His Word. It is not easy. Any lasting relationship takes time, commitment, and a willingness to lay down self. It is my prayer for you that Jesus will become your intimate companion of the journey that you are on. There will be laughter, tears, joy, and heartache but above all, there will be a Companion Who will walk with you and tell you the secrets that are on His heart. He will never leave you and will delight in you during your weak times and during your invincible times. You have a wonderful journey ahead and it is my prayer that you will walk through life with the most important treasure—intimacy with Jesus. You are a Warrior Princess, a "super girl" with extraordinary and special abilities and powers, but I pray you will see yourself ultimately as God's girl—invincible and uniquely cherished because you really know the King. May you fly with wings as an eagle and may all the dreams in your heart come true.

Baby girl, you've got this!

Hugs and blessings,

Cheryl

Endnotes

1 "800 Pacos." Bits & Pieces, October 15, 1992, p. 13. https://bible.org/illustration/800-pacos.

2 Greek and Hebrew keywords mentioned in this book are from *The Hebrew-Greek Key Study Bible* edited by Spiros Zodhiates.

3 From *The Hiding Place*, by Corrie Ten Boom.

4 This quote is attributed to Vivian Greene.

5 From page 4 of *Who Switched Off My Brain?* by Dr Caroline Leaf.

6 See page 35 of *Switch On Your Brain* by Dr Caroline Leaf.

7 See "Harvard cracks DNA storage, crams 700 terabytes of data into a single gram," Extreme Tech. http://www.extremetech.com/extreme/134672-harvard-cracks-dna-storage.

8 From page 8 of *The Prophetic Romance: A Study of the Book of Ruth* by Fuchsia Picket.

9 A compilation of the names of God from lists in Sylvia Gunter's Prayer Portion Series.

10 See *Boundaries: When to Say Yes, When to Say No, to Take Control of Your Life* by Henry Cloud and John Townsend.